Tyne Waters

A River and its Salmon

Carved in 1786 to adorn the newly built Somerset House in London,
this stone face is one of nine used to symbolise Britain's major rivers. The
head carries representations of the early Tyneside industries.

Tyne Waters

A River and its Salmon

Michael W. Marshall

H. F. & G. WITHERBY

For Julie and Sylvie

First published in Great Britain 1992
by H. F. & G. WITHERBY LTD,
14 Henrietta Street, London WC2E 8QJ

A catalogue record for this book is available from the
British Library

ISBN 0 85493 195 3

Typeset by CentraCet, Cambs
and printed and bound in Great Britain by
Butler and Tanner Ltd, Frome, Somerset

Contents

		Page
Picture Acknowledgements		6
Acknowledgements		7
Chapter 1	*Newcastle Salmon*	9
Chapter 2	*The Killing of the Tidal Tyne: 1800–1930*	27
Chapter 3	*A Managed, Cleaner, Salmon River*	57
Chapter 4	*Anglers on the Main Tyne*	81
Chapter 5	*The Lead Dales*	111
Chapter 6	*The Source*	129
Select Bibliography		155
Appendix	*Where to Fish*	157
Index		158

Picture Acknowledgements

Frontispiece from *The History and Antiquities of the Town and County of Newcastle upon Tyne*, J. Brand (1789); pages 14, 32, 45, 62/3, 65, 69, 70, 71, 74, 116, 121, 122, 126, 127, 132, 138, 141, 145 © Laurie Sparham; pages 84, 85, 87, 100/1, 125, 151, 152, 152/3 © M. W. Marshall; pages 29, 36/7, 48, 54/5 Gateshead Central Library; pages 23, 24/5, 31, 39, 52/3, 66, 67, 143 Newcastle University Library; page 9, 12, 27, 57, 81, 111, 129 from *The Tyne and its Tributaries*, W. J. Palmer (1882); pages 93, 94 from *A Fisher's Garland*, J. A. Harbottle (1904); page 98 from *Letters to a Salmon Fisher's Sons*, A. H. Chaytor (1910); page 103 from *Post Meridiana: Afternoon Essays*, H. Maxwell (1895); pages 146, 147 from *The Borders and Beyond*, A. Chapman (1924)

Acknowledgements

I would like to thank those, too numerous to mention, who gave their time to yarn about the river.

I would also like to thank the staff and representatives of the Gateshead Central Library, Hancock Museum, *Hexham Courant*, Newcastle Chronicle & Journal Ltd., Newcastle City Libraries, Newcastle University Library, Newcastle Literary and Philosophical Society, Northumberland County Record Office, Northumbrian Water (Rivers Division), National Rivers Authority, Northumbria Region, and the Northumbrian Anglers' Federation for being so helpful.

I am especially grateful to the following for valuable discussions and their time spent reading draft manuscripts:

R. Adams, the late M. Atkinson, M. Bishop, R. J. W. Coleby, P. Davis, Constance Fraser, P. Gray, G. Hall, I. McCredie, M. Macklin, J. Morrison Bell, K. Muter, A. Piper, W. Stokoe, K. Walker, W. Walker, J. Watson, A. Wallace, J. Wilkinson and N. Tortice. Any errors are, of course, my responsibility.

Special thanks are due to Mrs R. Baker, Ms C. Dubois, Ms J. Hinves for their critical comments during the preparation of the book. Also to my brother Peter, whose encouragement is always there. I would also like to thank David Burnett for seeing the book through the press.

The maps and drawings are by the late T. Telford, and Laurie Sparham took some wonderful photographs (see Picture Acknowledgements).

Black middens.

The Water of Tyne

I cannot get to my love if I would dee,
The water of Tyne runs between him and me,
And here I must stand with the tear in my e'e,
Both sighing and sickly my sweetheart to see.

O where is the boatman? my bonny hinny!
O where is the boatman? bring him to me,
To ferry me over the Tyne to my honey,
And I will remember the boatman and thee.

O bring me a boatman, I'll give any money,
And you for your trouble rewarded shall be,
To ferry me over the Tyne to my honey,
Or scull him across the rough river to me.

from Laura Alexandrine Smith

Chapter 1

NEWCASTLE SALMON

For thousands upon thousands of years, in a cycle older than recorded time, Tyne salmon have come back to their native river. These beautiful fish have survived a violent border history, and an industrial revolution that was to change the world. Tyne waters have reverberated with the measured tread of the Roman legions, the clash of Angle and Saxon, the shouts of plundering Vikings and reivers, the thunder of mounted Scottish and English knighthood, the cries of the river boatmen and the heavy thud of the steam hammers of Tyneside.

Each year silver smolts spawned on the gravel redds of the upper Tyne have swarmed down to the sea, to grow rapidly into grilse and salmon, building muscle and laying down fat for the return to their freshwater breeding grounds. More than five hundred generations of salmon have returned to the Tyne since the Romans first forded the river but, in the 1950s, the cycle was almost broken. The cold peaty waters of the source were turned by industrial Tyneside into a poisonous sludge and each year thousands of migrating smolts were killed as they tried to swim through this open sewer to the sea. Some miraculously survived, the cycle continued, and today, as a result of a massive clean-up campaign, salmon are returning to the river in ever-increasing numbers.

Tyne waters are capable of holding thousands of salmon: the area drained by the river is estimated to be over 1000 square miles. There are two major branches in the system – the North and South Tynes. The headwaters of the North Tyne are near the Scottish border and they flow off Windy Knowe, Peel and Deadwater Fells. Salmon once bred in the burns up on these fells – Bell's, Deadwater and Kielder – but now their redds are empty of returning salmon. A high dam, and Bakethin and Kielder reservoirs, have blocked their path.

The North Tyne flows out of the dam-face of Kielder Reservoir, one of the largest man-made lakes in Europe, and continues for over 40 miles to its confluence with the South Tyne. The South Tyne rises within a few miles of Cross Fell, flows past the towns of Alston and Haltwhistle and, fed by its major tributaries, the Nent and Allen, also travels nearly 40 miles from its source to meet the North Tyne. The two rivers join above Hexham to form the main Tyne which flows over 17 miles to Hedwin Streams, near Ryton, the traditional end of the tidal reaches. A major tributary, the Devil's Water, enters the main Tyne before Corbridge. There are 20 miles of tidal Tyne and its brackish waters are fed by the Derwent near Swalwell, the Team at Dunston, the Ouseburn at Newcastle and the Don near Jarrow. Today few salmon run up these tributaries to breed, as their paths are blocked by old barrages and weirs.

There is some suggestion that late Stone-Age men made regular summer migrations to the Tyne valleys where perhaps they harvested the returning salmon for food. There is no evidence that the Romans took salmon from the river, but after their invasion of Britain in AD 43 they saw salmon in the Thames, Severn and Trent, and named the fish *salmo* – the leaper. Salmon were almost certainly in the Tyne, since they travelled the same migration routes along Britain's coast as the Thames salmon.

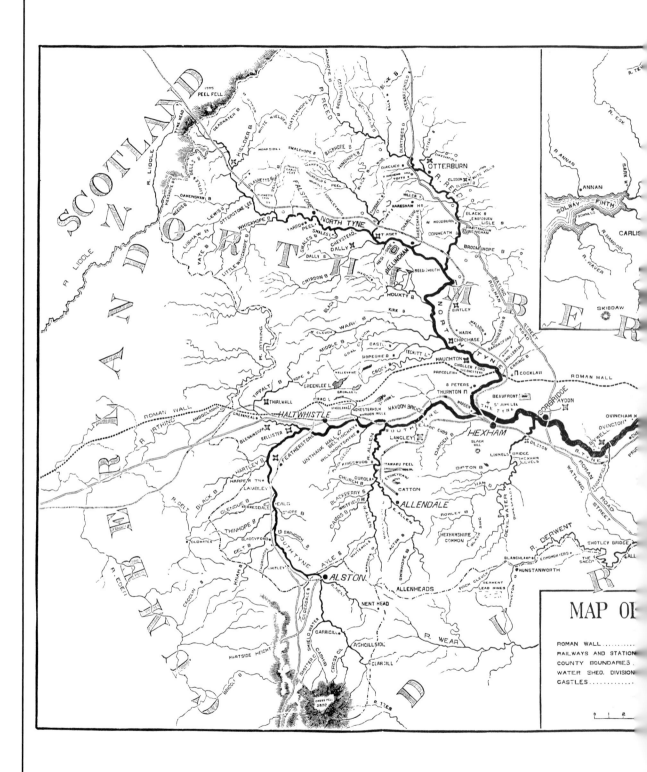

The Tyne and its tributaries, c. 1882.

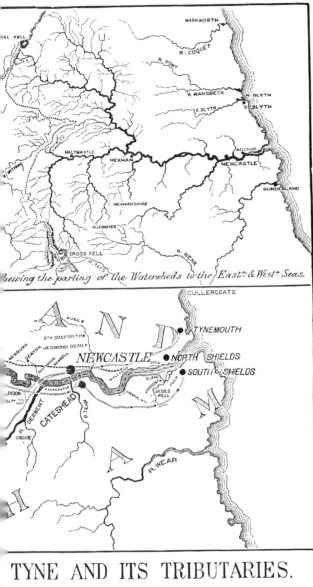

...ewing the parting of the Watersheds to the East & West Seas.

TYNE AND ITS TRIBUTARIES.

	CAMPS	o
	CHURCHES	+
	ROADS	
	TOWNS	●
	TOWERS	n

SCALE OF MILES.

The Roman legions first arrived on the banks of the Tyne in the AD 80s, under the command of Julius Agricola, and consolidated their position along the Tyne–Solway gap before pushing north into Scotland. Along the tributaries and valleys of the waters of the Tyne, they built bridges, fords, roads, forts and camps, and they created a pattern of settlements that is the basis of many modern towns and villages. Agricola probably built the original forts at Corbridge and Carlisle and the road that linked them, the Stanegate. (Stanegate was the name given to the Roman road in the Middle Ages, and meant 'stone road'.) It was probably also in Agricola's time that Roman engineers built a bridge near present-day Corbridge to carry Dere Street, the main supply route from York, across the Tyne, and there they built a fort to guard the bridge.

The Romans may have called the Tyne 'Tinea' (Rivet and Smith). A map of Britain drawn by Ptolemy in about AD 100 shows a northern river and names it 'Verda', but it is unclear if this river is the Tyne or the Wear. The Revd John Brand, in his *History of Newcastle* (1789), wrote: 'The present appellation of this river is implied in the first accounts of a religious house at Tinmouth, evidently so called from its vicinity to the mouth of the Tyne, which was first erected a little after the beginning of the seventh century.'

The Roman emperor Hadrian came to the Tyne in AD 122, and decided to define the northern limit of the Empire by building a wall along the Tyne–Solway gap to keep out 'the barbarians', and between AD 122 and AD 128 the IInd, VIth and XXth legions built the 85-mile-long Hadrian's Wall. It was constructed partly of stone and partly of turf, and when finished had 16 major forts, a number of smaller forts and a system of signalling stations.

Hadrian's great project was begun by bridging

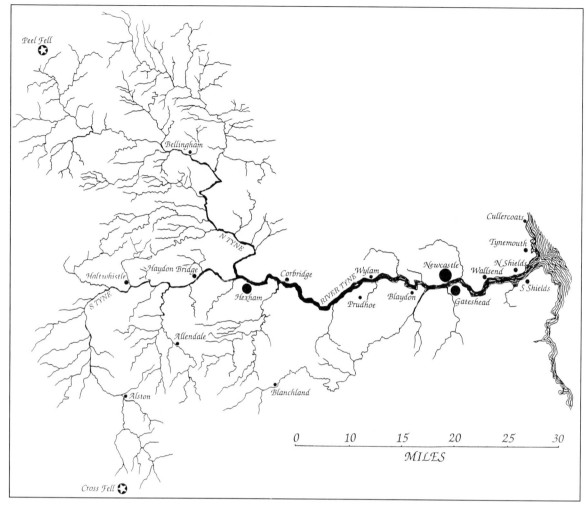

the Tyne near the mouth of a small stream, the Lort Burn. The Tyne was then a shallower, wider river than it is now and the Romans spanned it with a magnificent stone bridge – perhaps over 730 feet long and some 20 feet wide, its walkway supported by ten stone piers, each with an upstream and downstream cutwater. It was called Pons Aelius, or the Aelian Bridge, since 'Aelius' was Emperor Hadrian's family name. A nearby fort, which took its name from the bridge, was eventually to become the site of a Norman castle and the city of Newcastle upon Tyne.

In AD 123 the Roman VIth legion sailed from Germany and entered Britain via the River Tyne. The legionaries built a shrine on the completed bridge to the sea-gods Neptune and Oceanus – perhaps to give thanks for their safe passage across the North Sea.

Pons Aelius was the first of a series of bridges that crossed the Tyne at or close to the same site. The Roman bridge lasted perhaps nearly 1000 years. In 1072 the river was in heavy flood when

The Tyne after Kielder Dam.

William the Conqueror's army, on its way back from Scotland, was unable to cross the Tyne by a bridge – Pons Aelius may have been finally washed away. In 1080 the Normans may have rebuilt Pons Aelius or even constructed a new bridge. It is known that in 1248 Newcastle and its bridge were destroyed by fire. A new bridge was built in 1250 and this medieval bridge, perhaps built with the stone from Pons Aelius, lasted for over five hundred years before being swept away.

The Revd Brand wrote:

On the Saturday night preceding the 17th November, 1771, a great land flood, occasioned by heavy rains in the west . . . At Newcastle upon Tyne, the water began to rise about eleven o'clock at night, and continued increasing in height til seven the next morning: about three o'clock, the arches of this bridge were filled up, and between three and four, two of them on the south side were driven down, as was the North arch, adjoining to the toll shop, burying the houses erected thereon, together with several of their inhabitants.

The bridge was finally rebuilt in 1781. When the Victorian engineers were building Newcastle's present-day Swing Bridge they found, along with the VIth legion's altars, wooden piles, iron-capped stakes and the foundations of a medieval stone pier.

Pons Aelius fort was built probably in the late second or third century to guard the bridge and protect the little harbour in the Tyne off the Lort Burn. Hadrian's Wall was to have ended at Newcastle, but while it was under construction the Romans decided to extend it to Wallsend (Segedunum).

A fort was built at the mouth of the Tyne at present-day South Shields, possibly by Agricola. Hadrian built a fort (Arbeia) on The Lawe, and the settlement at South Shields became an important harbour for Roman ships. Riverside quays must have been constructed by the Roman commanders, whose various military campaigns relied heavily on sea transport for support.

Hadrian's Wall was continued west from Pons Aelius along the valley of the main Tyne. Major forts were built at Benwell (Condercum), at Rudchester (Vindbola) north of present-day Wylam, and at Halton (Hunnum). The fort at Corbridge, built near the bridge, played an important military role in the Roman occupation of northern Britain. The Roman bridge (which was upstream of today's bridge at Corbridge) had stone piers and eleven openings, and the bridge masonry, remains of which can still be seen in the river, was held in place with iron cramps coated with lead – iron for strength and lead to resist corrosion.

The Wall passed north of Corbridge and crossed the North Tyne near a fort on the west bank of the river at Chesters (Cilurnum), just downstream of the present-day bridge at Chollerford. It was carried across the river on massive pillars that were probably specially designed to constrict the river and increase flow rates to prevent attackers from passing underneath the arches. There were four openings, the piers were 50 feet apart (centre to centre) and the cutwaters were built on the upstream sides of the piers. The North Tyne has changed its course and left some well-preserved remnants of the bridge high and dry on its east bank.

The three major Roman bridges across the Tyne (Chesters, Corbridge and Pons Aelius) probably did not have stone arches, their roadways being carried on timber beams supported by the stone piers. From Chesters, the Wall was taken via Fort Carrawburgh (Brocolitia) to another fort at Housesteads (Vercovicium), which was situated behind the Wall. At Housesteads a beautiful sculpture of a reclining Neptune was found. Neptune, in addition to being a sea-god, was the Roman god of flowing water, springs, streams and fountains. In 1882, in his book *The Tyne and its Tributaries*, W. J. Palmer drew the Housesteads Neptune. He called it 'Supposed Roman Sculpture of River God of North Tyne' and underneath quoted Wordsworth:

Here thou mayst perceive
The local deity with oozy hair
And mineral crown beside his jagged urn
Recumbent. Him thou mayst behold, who
   hides
His lineaments by day, yet there presides,
Teaching the docile waters how to turn;
Or, if need be, impediment to spurn,
And force their passage to the salt sea tides.

Roman soldiers, whilst building the Tyne bridges, garrisoning the forts or on patrol, could have fished for salmon. Perhaps they speared them with lance and trident, or cast nets from boat or bank. Legions garrisoned in France (Gaul) knew how to catch salmon at this time. Pliny the Elder, who died during the eruption of Versuvius in AD 79, wrote in his *Historia Naturalis* that 'in Aquitaine the river salmon is preferred to all sea fish'.

The Romans certainly used fish-hooks, perhaps tempting Tyne salmon with worms. There is some evidence that they fished with artificial flies in other rivers. But the forts and settlements along the Tyne have yet to reveal Roman fishing methods. However, that the Romans fished British rivers 'no doubt strenuously in the vicinity of the large settlements, there is no reason to question, and a remarkable antefix (eaves tile) from York shows a fisherman with net and trap. York also may have evidence of preparation of fish on a large scale (for sauce?) in the late fourth

century.' (Hartley and Fitts.)

The earliest recorded watermen on the Tyne were the Barcarii Tigrisienses from the Tigris in Mesopotamia. They arrived in the AD 300s, and perhaps ferried stores in a local version of the giant coracles that were in use on their home river. Alternatively they may have used specially built barges to carry cargo from the quays at South Shields to the forts along the Tyne.

The Romans were successful in holding the northern outposts of their empire for well over 250 years, and Corbridge was still a flourishing settlement in the late fourth century. In a letter written in AD 410, the Roman emperor Honorius disowned Britain and left the Tyne valleys to their fate. The many peaceful, unprotected Romano-British settlements were easy prey to the fierce incoming Irish, Scottish and German tribes.

During the fifth century tribes from lower Germany, the Angles (along with the Saxons and Jutes), invaded and settled along the east and north-east coast of Britain to create Angleland, or England. In 547 a warrior band of Angles, led by Ida, travelled up by sea from Yorkshire and landed at Bamburgh, north of the River Tyne. They settled there, developed a stronghold and set about creating the kingdom of Bernicia that was to stretch from the banks of the River Tyne to the Firth of Forth. Ida's grandson Aethelfrith created Northumbria from Bernicia and the neighbouring kingdom of Deira, and Northumbria became the most important political and cultural centre in seventh-century England. It is hard to believe that Pons Aelius, which would have been the link across the Tyne between Bernicia and Deira, did not play an important role in the development of Northumbria; but there is little evidence to suggest that there was even a significant Anglo-Saxon settlement at Pons Aelius.

During the seventh and eighth centuries,

Northumbrian Christian monasteries and culture flourished. Monasteries were built on the banks of the Tyne at Hexham, Corbridge, Gateshead, Jarrow and Tynemouth. The Venerable Bede lived in the Jarrow monastery from 682, and produced his famous *Ecclesiastical History of the English People*, an important study of Anglo-Saxon history. He wrote that 'Britain is remarkable for . . . its rivers, which abound in fish, particularly salmon.' No doubt he included the Tyne, along whose banks he walked daily.

By the end of the ninth century Northumbria's power had declined as the kingdom was threatened on three fronts, by Saxons, Vikings and Scots. The West Saxons pushed north into Northumbria under Egbert, king of Wessex. The Vikings' longships probably first entered the Tyne in 787, and seven years later they returned to sack and loot the Jarrow monastery. The Viking leader was lost in the skirmish, and some of his longships sank when they went aground on Herd Sands at the river mouth. But the Norsemen returned in earnest in 875, when Halfdan brought a fleet of longships into the Tyne. Tynemouth monastery was attacked and looted before Halfdan settled down to winter on a river island, possibly at the confluence with the Don at Jarrow Slake. In the following spring, the Vikings laid waste much of Northumbria: Lindisfarne and Hexham monasteries were burnt and looted and the remaining monks massacred. The new kingdom of Scotland, formed when the Picts and Scots united in 844, became a formidable and long-lasting threat to Northumbria, and by the 960s the Scots had pushed down almost to the Tyne, destroying most of Northumbria, which declined from a kingdom into an earldom.

Amidst the general devastation caused by the Vikings the Northumbrian monastery on Lindisfarne was abandoned and eventually transferred to Durham. The pious Anglo-Saxon kings and notables of Northumbria gradually gave all their land between the Tyne and Tees rivers to the bishop and church of Durham.

After the Norman Conquest, the church and lands of Durham were detached from the earldom of Northumbria and given to the bishop, who also had control over Durham Cathedral and Durham Castle. By the Middle Ages the bishop of Durham held an extremely powerful position; he levied taxes, raised troops, had his own mint, a hunting ground, the right to all treasure trove on his extensive lands and control over rich coal and lead mines. The priory and the bishop of Durham played a key role in the evolution of the settlements on the south bank of the Tyne, and for centuries there were disputes between the developing and increasingly important town of Newcastle and the priory and bishop. There were constant arguments over the control of navigation rights on the river, the bridge at Newcastle, and the export of coal from mines at Gateshead and Whickham.

Newcastle's importance dates from 1080, fourteen years after the Norman Conquest, when a 'New Castle' of wood and earth was built by William the Conqueror's son Robert on the site of the Roman fort at Pons Aelius. After the Normans had secured Cumberland and built Carlisle Castle the Tyne–Solway gap came under their control. New Castle with its bridge over the Tyne quickly became a strategic centre: a castle where armies could be gathered and supplied by sea and road, and where military expeditions could be organised. After 1168 the Normans rebuilt New Castle in stone, and traders and merchants gathered round its walls for protection – Newcastle was there to stay. Around 1200 stone-faced, clay-filled jetties were built in the river and the Tyne began to play an increasingly important role in Newcastle's growth, in a period when the Roman roads sank into disrepair and sea transport became the most important means of communication.

In medieval times it was important for developing towns to be given royal charters (and other formal documents) so as to obtain trading monopolies. Newcastle has no founding charter, but was a borough – that is, a fortified town with special rights and privileges. Newcastle's earliest known charter is dated 1175, in the reign of Henry II, and by it the town's burgesses were acquitted, amongst other things, from paying a toll for use of the Tyne. Throughout the centuries Newcastle burgesses fought hard to keep their trading monopolies and control over trade and navigation on the Tyne. In the 1300s, for example, they tried to prevent ships from mooring on the south side of the river and fish from being landed at South Shields. In 1352 the mayor and burgesses of Newcastle even went as far as to seize South Shields fishing boats and, after carrying them to Newcastle, forced the owners to swear that in future they would only sell fish at the Newcastle fish market!

It is almost certain that throughout the Dark Ages salmon were returning to the Tyne to spawn, but there is little evidence to prove it. But by the Middle Ages contemporary documents make specific references to the Tyne salmon fisheries, and a recent excavation of Newcastle's medieval quayside found evidence of salmon bones. The earliest fisheries on the Tyne were often referred to as 'yares', and were specific sites or stations where nets were probably hung from stakes set into the river bank and bed. (A yare or 'yair' generally means some sort of enclosure for catching fish, while a yare net was the long net that was held in place by the stakes.) It was probably soon discovered that nets rowed out into

the Tyne from the sterns of small boats were a more productive method of catching salmon than fixed nets. One ancient variety of boat fishing with a net is 'wear-shot' fishing, where the net is rowed out and back from the shore in a large circle (the circle's size is limited by the net's length) and then retrieved by men stationed on the shore.

At the beginning of the twelfth century the bishop of Durham used the Tyne salmon fisheries to support his claim to 'one moiety' of the river. Since, he argued, fishermen were fishing from his land on the south bank of the Tyne at some 20 fisheries, he had thus established his right to a moiety extending from the south side. He was successful in his claim. The other moiety, extending from the north side of the river, was given to the earl and county of Northumberland. The middle of the Tyne was to remain 'common and free' for shipping.

There were plenty of salmon in the River Tyne throughout the twelfth century. A bishop's charter to the prior and monks of Durham, dating from 1103, mentions 28 salmon fisheries, eight on the north bank in the parishes of Tynemouth and Wallsend, and 20 on the south bank in the parish of Jarrow. In an inquisition (inquiry) during the reign of Henry II (1154–89) there was mention of salmon fisheries along the main Tyne from Jarrow to Hedwin Streams (near present-day Ryton) in the parishes of Gateshead, Whickham and Ryton. Forty of the fisheries were the property of the bishop of Durham, and there were 'no less than 68 fisheries on the south side of the river from Hedwin Streams down to the sea' (Gutherie, 1880).

In about 1180 the bishop of Durham set up a leper hospital near Durham at Sherburn. Here inmates were to be given a loaf of bread and a daily ration of beer with fish on three days of the week and meat on the other four. On 'great festivals' special dishes were provided, and at the feast of St Cuthbert in Lent (20 March) fresh salmon – if available.

In the year 1285 the Tyne, together with other northern rivers, came under the protection of an Act establishing a close season for mature salmon and smolts:

> *It is provided that the waters of Humber, Ouse, Trent, Don, Aire, Derwent, Wharfe, Nid, Ure, Swale, Tees, Tyne, Eden and all other waters wherein salmon be taken, shall be in defence for taking salmons from the Nativity of our Lady [8 September] unto St Martin's Day [11 November], and that likewise young salmons shall not be taken nor destroyed by nets, nor by other engines at millpools from the midst of April unto the Nativity of St John Baptist [24 June]. And in places where such water banks are there shall be assigned overseers of this statute, which, being sworn, shall oftentimes see and inquire of the offenders; and for the first trespass they shall be punished by burning of their nets and engines, and for the second they shall have imprisonment for a quarter of a year; and for the third they shall be imprisoned for a whole year; and as their trespass increaseth so shall the punishment.*

In 1323 there was an inquisition at Gateshead that mentions three Tyne fisheries, called Greneyard and belonging to the bishop of Durham, 'which had been broken down to the length of 24 perches' (Welford; one perch = 5½ yards or 5.029 metres). In 1335 the prior of Tynemouth leased the Elstewykyare (Elswick) fishery for three years at a yearly rent of £6 13s. 4d. The agreement insisted that the priory had to be supplied with two salmon during Lent.

In 1345 a commission was issued by the bishop of Durham to the prior of Durham to make

'inquisition as to persons who have unlawfully interfered with his rights of navigation and fishing in the southern half of the waters of the Tyne'. The bishop repeated his claim that from 'time beyond the memory of man', there existed

> *a fishery near Ryton called the Blaklough, to the westward of Tyne Bridge, belonging to the bishopric; another called Cromwell, of which the third part belonged to the see; another called Qickham Drawwater, belonging to the bishop; a yare called the Rutyare, which also belonged to the see, and used to extend to the mid-water of Tyne; another yare of like extent, called Maleyare, near the Redheugh – all west of Tyne Bridge; and on the east of the bridge the Kirkyare, beneath the bishop's manor at Gateshead extending to one-third part of the water of Tyne; a fishery called Toulershell, and a yare under Gateshead park called Helperyare; and lastly a fishery called Turnwater, under Freregose (Friars' Goose), belonging to the bishop. (Welford.)*

It is almost certain that these were salmon and sea-trout fisheries situated in brackish water miles from the sea. In such places, there would have been few species worth catching other than migratory fish.

Throughout most of its history, from the Norman Conquest onwards, trade and industry at Newcastle prospered, usually at the expense of other towns on the Tyne, so that Newcastle gave rise to two world-famous proverbs – both dealing with exports from the Tyne. Of the two, the medieval proverb is less well known: 'A Scot, a rat and a Newcastle grindstone may be found all the world over.' Newcastle grindstones would have come from stony ridges around Tyneside. The coal that it would be pointless to carry to Newcastle came from mines on the river's north and south banks. Coal had been mined on Tyneside since Roman times and the industry was well established by the thirteenth century, exports probably first occurring from Tynemouth. The prior of Tynemouth owned mines at Elswick and Benwell and the bishop of Durham at Gateshead and Whickham. Incredibly, in 1357 the Newcastle burgesses persuaded King Edward III to order that coals taken from the bishop's Gateshead mines should first be taken by boat to Newcastle, whence only after paying a Newcastle custom charge could they be exported.

In the Middle Ages the supremacy of the original major exports from the Tyne, wool and leather, was being challenged by coal, lead, grindstones and salt. Before the use of ice in the late eighteenth century, salting and smoking were the only means of salmon preservation. Since 1225 Tynemouth monastery had been developing a fishing port on the north banks of the Tyne at North Shields to replace the 'shiels' or simple huts inhabited by the local fishermen. Salt for salmon pickling and preserving would probably have been obtained from the opposite bank of the river where South Shields had built up a thriving salt-making industry. Sea water was piped in from the river at high tide and South Shields 'salters' would evaporate the brine using coal fires lit under huge flat pans made of lead and later, in the 1400s, of iron. By the mid-1500s there were, in both North and South Shields, over 150 salt pans and the industry employed many salters and 'keelmen', who brought the coal from the up-river mines in their lighters or keels. In the 1600s, North Sea fishing vessels would arrive at Shields in their hundreds to load salt, but the industry declined in the mid-1700s when coal became more expensive and the natural Cheshire rock-salt deposits were found.

In 1400 Newcastle was granted a charter by Henry IV making the town a county in its own right, separate from Northumberland, and during the fifteenth century the Newcastle burgesses proposed, much to the displeasure of South Shields men, that, because of an ancient charter, ships in the Tyne could only be worked at Newcastle. The burgesses even complained to the bishop of Durham that he had 'built a town at South Shields where no town should be'! During Henry VIII's reign (1509–47) the burgesses complained that the prior of Tynemouth was daily loading and discharging ships at Tynemouth and Shields, thereby taking duties that belonged to the king. Further, the prior was making 'fyschgarthes [fishtraps] and weeres for takyn salmone' between Newcastle and the sea and each year removed them from place to place so that the port was 'wrekked and shallowed'. In 1529 a statute was passed decreeing that within the tidal limits of the Tyne all goods had to be loaded at Newcastle. This statute was only slightly modified by a royal charter of 1600 which allowed ships, if they were too large to sail up the Tyne to Newcastle, to load or unload at the river's mouth – a reference to the increasing shallowness of the Tyne and an indication that Shields was becoming an important harbour.

Salmon were in the Tyne in large numbers during the sixteenth century. The accounts of the bursar of Durham monastery for the years between 1530 and 1534 show that throughout each year enormous quantities of fresh and salted Tyne salmon (*salmonum salsorum*), grilse or young salmon (*gylsse*) and sea trout were being purchased by the priory. There are also records of many 'seaymes' of fresh salmon (a pack-horse load of fish, each 'seam' consisting of a dozen salmon) being transported from a salmon fishery at Ovingham, as well as accounts of the priory purchasing vast quantities of salted salmon.

Besides salmon the priory provisioned itself with eels, tench, pike, seals, seal calves and 'sea-pigs' (*porco marino*, dolphins).

'Fish and ring' stories were quite common in both the Middle East and the West in the sixteenth century. Newcastle's first local historian, Gray, wrote:

> There was a strange accident upon the bridge, hapned to an alderman of Newcastle, looking over the bridge into the river, with his hands over; his gould ring fell off his finger into the water; which was given for lost. It chanced that one of his servants bought a salmon in the market, opening the belly of the fish, found his master's ring in the guts. (Welford.)

The story is not impossible: recently it was reported that a salmon taken by an angler from the River Orchy had a 20p piece in its stomach.

In the sixteenth century angling was

> probably too tame for the hot-blooded Northumbrians . . . The fish were either caught with a net or with the leister (a trident-like spear). A Dr William Turner gives a vivid description of leister fishing: 'Fysshers in Northumberlande [he says] pyll of the vttermoste barke and put it in the clyft of a styke and set it in fire and hold it at the water syde and make fyshe cum thyther, which, if they se, they stryke withe their leysters or sammon spears.' (Tomlinson, 1897.)

By the end of the Middle Ages, the burgesses of Newcastle had secured almost complete control of coal production on Tyneside. In 1600 a charter from Elizabeth I to the mayor and burgesses gave the Newcastle Company of Hostmen (coal merchants) the right to load coal at any point on the Tyne. In the seventeenth century coal was mined mainly on the bishop's land on the south side of the river at Gateshead, Whickham,

Ryton, Winlaton and Stella, and even though these mines were not located in Newcastle their coal was still known as 'Newcastle coal'. But there were also mines in the Newcastle area at, for example, Elswick, Benwell, Denton, Fenham and Walker. By 1606, Newcastle had gained complete power over the navigation and conservancy of the River Tyne when the Admiralty gave the burgesses the right to control the Port of Tyne from 'Hedwin Streams to Spar Hawk' (Spar Hawk was off the river mouth).

Despite Newcastle's being a royalist stronghold in the Civil War (1642–51), the Puritans who took over Newcastle Corporation were just as jealous of the town's trading rights as the royalist burgesses they replaced, continuing to keep the towns of North and South Shields in subordination to Newcastle. Ralph Gardiner of Chirton, for example, in an attempt to establish trading rights for North Shields, wrote *England's Grievances Discovered, in relation to the coal trade* (1655), wherein he charged Newcastle Corporation with 'tyranny and oppression'. Gardiner was unsuccessful in breaking Newcastle's hold on the river, but he did publish a beautiful map of the Tyne showing, perhaps with bias, 'North and South Sheelds' harbours crammed with ships while Newcastle quays are almost deserted.

Despite the rise of riverside industries and increased river traffic during the eighteenth century, the Tyne was still a prodigious salmon water. In 1725 Daniel Defoe recorded that each year London received a great quantity of pickled or cured salmon known as 'Newcastle salmon', though 'upon enquiry', he discovered that although some came from Newcastle, most was taken as far away as the Tweed and brought overland by horse to be pickled and cured at Shields. Exports from the Tyne in 1782 were

'coals, lead, glass, salt, although this trade is
almost lost, grindstones, cinders'. Other products
were tallow, butter and salmon – 'for which there
is a great many fisheries on the river which
produce immense quantities' (Brand). But Brand
is in agreement with Defoe that the greatest
quantity of salmon was shipped from Berwick as
'Newcastle salmon': 'for anciently they were
brought to Newcastle by land-carriage and being
shipped from this port were called, with the fish
really caught in this river, by the common name
of Newcastle salmon in London'.

   The eighteenth-century Tyne fisheries were
enormously productive and salmon, always a
luxury fish, continued to fetch good prices. On 12
June 1755 over 2400 salmon were taken in a
fishery above Newcastle bridge, and these were
sold at Newcastle market for 1d. and 1¼d. a
pound. Three years later, on 20 July, more than
2000 salmon were taken in the river. On 29 May
1760 a huge salmon was netted in the Tyne and
sold in the Newcastle market for 11s. It weighed
54 lb., was 4 feet 4 inches long and 33 inches
round. On 6 August 1761, 260 salmon were taken
in the Tyne at the Newburn fishery 'in one
draught' (Sykes). (The use of the term 'draught'
suggests that salmon were being fished from boats,
perhaps with the wear-shot net technique.) Three
years later, on 14 May, the same Newburn fishery
caught many large salmon and probably the longest
salmon ever caught in the Tyne – 5½ feet long, 28
inches round and weighing 54 lb. On 29 June 1765,
144 large salmon were taken in one draught at the
Shields fishery near the bar at the river mouth, and
on 15 July more than 4000 salmon were for sale at
Newcastle fish market for 1¼d. a pound. The
fishery above the Tyne Bridge caught 107 in the
morning of that day. On 9 June 1775 the Low
Lights fishery, near North Shields, caught 265
salmon in one draught (Sykes).

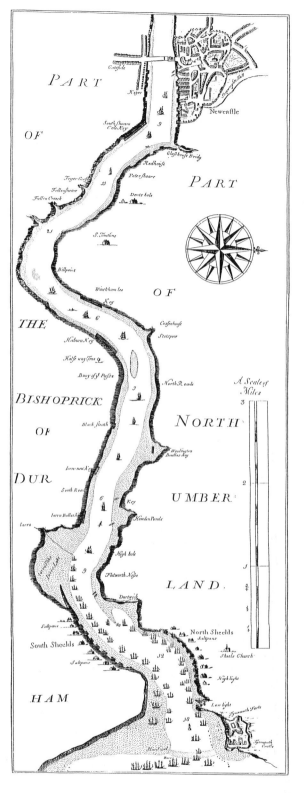

Gardiner's 1786 map of the lower Tyne.

Angling for Tyne salmon was certainly practised during the eighteenth century. By the second half of the seventeenth century Izaak Walton was advising on how to fish for salmon with worm, minnow or artificial fly, and described how many fished for salmon 'with a ring of wire on the top of their rod, through which the line may run to as great a length as is needful when he is hooked. And to that end, some use a wheel about the middle of their rod, or near the hand.' He also mentions the Northumberland bull-trout, 'of much greater length and bigness than any in the southern parts'.

Thomas Bewick, the famous Tyneside wood engraver, was a keen fisherman, a champion of the salmon angler and an active salmon conservationist. Born in 1753 on the banks of the

Cherryburn, a small stream that entered the main Tyne on its south bank opposite and between the villages of Ovington and Ovingham, Bewick started fishing at an early age. Robert Robinson, his biographer, quotes one of Bewick's childhood recollections:

as soon as the bushes and trees began to put forth their buds, and make the face of Nature look gay, this was signal for the angler to prepare his fishing tackle. In doing this I was not behind. Fishing rods, set-gads and night lines were all soon made fit for use, and with them, late and early, I had a busy time of it during the summer months, until the frosts of autumn forbade me to proceed.

When Bewick was young, Tyne salmon were plentiful. He wrote:

A John W. Carmichael (1800–68) engraving of the salmon fishery at Dent's Hole, one of the few deep-water mooring holes in the Tyne. Drawn from the north bank about a mile downstream of the Ouseburn, c. 1825. Note the keels and colliers in the background.

Woodcuts of the Tyne by local artist Thomas Bewick (1759–1828).

When a boy, from about the year 1760 to 1767, I was frequently sent by my parents to the fishermen at Eltringham Ford to purchase a salmon, and was always desired not to pay 2d. a pound, and I commonly paid only a 1d. and sometimes 1½d. Before, or perhaps about that time, I had been told that an article had always been inserted in every indenture of apprenticeship in Newcastle, that the apprentices were not forced to eat salmon above twice a week, and the same bargain was made with the common servants.

But salmon have always been a luxury fish, and the tales of 'salmon and apprentice indentures' – tales that have been handed down from generation to generation – are now thought to be false. 'The myth is current of Edinburgh, Newcastle as well as London apprentices' indentures . . . I share with Mr Cohen, whose lucid study should be consulted, the belief that there never was such a clause in apprentices' indentures.' (Wheeler.)

For much longer than these 1800 years of history salmon must have travelled up the Tyne, to its tributaries and small burns, to spawn. But soon the rise of nineteenth-century industrial Tyneside was to decimate the salmon runs and, for a while, in the mid-twentieth century, the salmon almost disappeared as the river died.

Dredger on the River Tyne.

Nae mair we'll fish the coolly Tyne
Nae mair tho oozy Team.

from 'The Coaly Tyne'

Chapter 2

THE KILLING OF THE TIDAL TYNE: 1800–1930

A s the industrial revolution accelerated, machines turned from water to steam power and coal was needed in ever-increasing amounts. Tyneside, situated in the heart of the huge Northumberland and Durham coalfields, supplied the need. Around 1800 coal prices began to soar; new pits were opened and Newcastle coal exports rose dramatically – coal production boosted by new technology. As the nineteenth century progressed some old Tyneside industries – glass,

pottery, chemicals and iron – died and were replaced by the three mighty Victorian industries: coal, heavy engineering and shipbuilding.

The railways were a key factor in the evolution of industrial Britain, and Tyneside played a major role in their development. George Stephenson, born on the banks of the Tyne at Wylam, built the famous *Rocket*, which in 1829 reached the astounding speed of 36 miles per hour on the Liverpool and Manchester railway. Within the next 30 years a railway network was created that is the basis of our present system. In 1844 the last horse-drawn mail coach left Newcastle for London. The building of new bridges across the Tyne between Newcastle and Gateshead illustrates the growth of nineteenth-century industrial Tyneside. From the time of the Romans until the High Level Bridge was built in 1849 there had been only one bridge across the river at Newcastle. However, in 1831 a suspension bridge

The High Level Bridge and the old Newcastle Bridge, c. 1875.

had been built at nearby Scotswood, and in 1839 the first Scotswood railway bridge was constructed. After completion of Newcastle's High Level Bridge and another bridge across the Tweed in 1850 – both built by George Stephenson's son, Robert – Edinburgh was connected to Newcastle, and thus to London by rail. The Redheugh Bridge was built in 1871, and the low-arched Tyne Bridge was removed and replaced by a swing bridge in 1876. The King Edward Bridge was opened in 1906 by King Edward VII, and in 1928 the massive, graceful arches of Newcastle's most famous bridge, the Tyne Bridge, were completed. But as railways, industry and population grew, the tidal Tyne became increasingly polluted and the Newcastle salmon fisheries were soon to be no more.

Even in the early part of the nineteenth century, the Tyne salmon fisheries were not producing the same numbers of fish as they had in the previous century. Around 1807 salmon, instead of fetching about a 1d. a pound as they had in the 1760s, cost as much as 1s., 2s. or even 3s. 6d. a pound. A document written in 1802 complained:

> *There are many fisheries on the Tyne and in some seasons very productive . . . The fish are offered for sale on the Sandhill at the Maison Dieu; while the great part are pickled, kitted and exported many thousands in a season. But during the war the price has been so exorbitant . . . that, like the unbelieving Lord in the scripture, the people of Newcastle see it with their eyes, but do not taste it.*

The reduction in the number of salmon was attributed to various causes: the locks at Bywell and Winlaton mills that held up, or even prevented, the fish from ascending to their redds; the increase in the number of craft on the river

Swing bridge in the foreground, and the new Tyne Bridge, 1928.

and the 'deleterious mixtures that are carried into the stream from the lead-mines and various manufactories on the banks of the river' (Mackenzie, 1827); and poaching. The Tyne is listed as being one of England's principal salmon rivers in 1839; and yet in that year it was reported that 'very few salmon, comparatively speaking, are now taken on the Tyne', and that 'the Tyne, so long famous for its salmon fishery, has been greatly injured by the traffic at its mouth, and especially by the increase of steam-boats' (Hofland).

Nevertheless, during the first half of the nineteenth century salmon were still being caught by both net and rod – often big fish and in large numbers. Incredibly, a pair of spectacles in a steel case were taken out of the 'maw' of what must have been a very large salmon at Newcastle fish market on 12 October 1825 (Sykes). On another occasion, in 1833, between 400 and 500 salmon were brought to the Newcastle fish market to be sold and 'Newcastle salmon' were still being pickled in salt, put into boxes or kits, and exported to London. Stephen Oliver, a keen fly-fisherman, wrote in 1834 that the largest salmon he ever saw came from the Tyne and it weighed

Probable remains of the Bywell weir, taken from the north bank of the main Tyne.

48 lb., but it was probably taken in the nets.

In the first part of the nineteenth century angling was well established on Tyneside. For example, in April 1822 a Newcastle Waltonian Club was formed and their president William Mitchell read a paper on 27 July 1824 'On the Pleasure and Utility of Angling'. A regularly produced 'Newcastle Fisher's Garland' extolled the virtues of Tyne angling. One of many such garlands, 'The Angler's Delight', was written by Robert Nichol in 1820:

> When the sunbeams are bright in the far
>   eastern sky,
> The Angler departs with his rod, line and fly;
> Of the vice of the town nor its folly he dreams,
> For his soul is wrapp'd up in the sport of the
>   streams.
>
> A lunch in his pocket – a creel on his back,
> Up Tyneside he wanders, ne'er minding a
>   track;
> Though colour'd the water, and cloudy the sky,
> His mind's full of hope when he puts out the
>   fly . . .

Another local bard, William Thompson, produced 'The Tyne Fisher's Call' in 1830:

> The snow has left the verdant heights
> Which stand by rapid Tyne,
> And Spring invites the blithesome wights
> Who yield rod and line.
> The sun is glancing on the stream;
> The lav'rock seeks the sky;
> Then rouse from each lethargic dream,
> And forward, fishers, hie!
>
> . . .
>
> By Bywell's Tower and Prudhoe's steep,
> In ruin frowning grey,
> By shady Derwent, dark and deep,

> Secure the shining prey.
> Where Gibside's woods wave green in pride,
> Where Tanfields arch springs high;
> Swift, reach the rovers as they glide,
> And lure them as they lie . . .

In the 1830s, the Tyne was a

shallow stream, full of sandbanks and eccentric eddies, which at Newcastle, men might ford at low tide. It wended its peaceful course from the junction of the North and South Tyne above Hexham through a charming valley, whose gently undulating uplands showed here a swelling glade and rich pasture . . . Under the massive arches of Hexham Bridge, past the crumbling ruin of Prudhoe castle, meandering by (George) Stephenson's lonely cottage at Wylam, between the drooping willows at Ryton's shore, doubling Newburn haugh and stealing with quickened force on either side of King's Meadows, the rustic river sped on untrammelled and unstained till its waters darkened under the shadow of Newcastle Town . . . The Tyne, over what was then its navigable reach, twisted, turned, and expanded, now rushing with impetuous haste past the mid-stream projection of Bill Point . . . stretching its expanse over Jarrow Slake, only to gather fresh force for the sweep round Whitehill Point and the final charge through the 'Narrows' at Shields into the broad sea beyond. (Palmer.)

The mouth of the river was 'merely an exposed outlet of the river, flanked on the north side by the treacherous Black Middens and on the south side by the Herd Sand, while across its entrance the sea fretted across a bar which left but six feet of water at low tide.' (Johnson, 1895.)

Salmon arriving at the Tyne estuary in 1837, the year Queen Victoria came to the throne, entered a river without docks. They swam

ON FOLLOWING PAGES: *Carmichael's engraving of the north bank of the main Tyne, looking downstream from Ovingham, c. 1825. Prudhoe Castle is on the south bank.*

alongside the London-bound sailing colliers waiting at anchor for their cargoes in the deep-water holes in the main stream. The coal trade was sometimes referred to 'as the greatest nursery of seamen we have in England', and seamen who left the colliers for the navy liked Newcastle salmon. A contemporary account describes such a man:

> If his breeding has been North of Yarmouth, he is distinguished with the title of Collier's nag; and indeed he is a rare horse that will never fail you in bad Weather, being insensible to Rain, Cold or Thunder as a Cannon-Bullet. He is generally above the common size of other Tars, in Bulk, Strength and Courage, which is mainly owing to his northern Diet, which he thinks on with Heavy heart every time he sees a Coal Fire. He is a great Admirer of the North-country Beef and Pease-Pudding, yet allows Newcastle Ale and Salmon to be the most Superlative Diet in the Universe. (Ward, quoted by Davis.)

At Newcastle the salmon passed under a low-arched bridge that acted as a barrier to any tall-masted sailing ship. Coal had to be carried downstream from the mines and under the bridge to the sailing colliers in 'keels' – special lighters that had been operated by 'keelmen' since the 1300s. For centuries keels remained almost unchanged: heavy, wide-beamed and pointed at both ends. They were around 40 feet long and were sailed, punted and rowed by a crew of four men and a boy.

A Society of Keelmen was instituted at Newcastle, perhaps as early as 1516. Their employers were the Hostmen, who had the monopoly of coal-carrying on the Tyne, thus making the keelmen a powerful body. In 1771 the keelmen went on strike in protest at the building of 'staithes' near Shields where coal could be gravity-loaded direct from wagons into the sailing

Pelaw main staithes (coal drops) at Bill Quay, c. 1900. Lighters, colliers and three-island tramp ships can be seen in the foreground, and in the background steam dredgers and shipyards.

'colliers brigs'. The strike was successful, and it was not until the early 1820s that staithes were built in the lower reaches. By the mid- to late nineteenth century, after the rapid introduction of the railways, staithes were to be found at North and South Shields, at Hay Hole, at Wallsend and at Pelaw; coal wagons, after being placed in cradles, were bodily lowered down to the collier and coal dropped out of bottom doors in the wagons directly into the ships' holds. Later coal was loaded directly from wagons that discharged into one of a number of chutes, each with a different outlet or 'spout' so that loading could take place at any state of the tide. The widespread introduction of coal staithes marked the end of the Tyne keels. Their passing marked another step in the industrialisation of the Tyne that was eventually to take the salmon runs to the brink of destruction.

The bluff-bowed, wooden-hulled nineteenth-century collier or 'Geordie brig', with its three headsails, two masts, each square-rigged with a mainsail and a topsail, and an additional fore and aft spanker on the second mast, was doomed when the first iron-hulled, screw-driven collier, the *John Bowes*, was launched in 1852 from Palmer's yard at Jarrow on Tyne. The *John Bowes* was launched with the new 'double-bottom tanks' that were built into the underwater section of the hull. Double-bottom tanks had one big advantage: they could be filled with water for ballast. Before a collier's return voyage the double-bottom tanks were flooded with sea water which, on arrival at Newcastle, could be easily pumped over the side to lighten the ship for loading. For centuries Newcastle colliers had sailed outward from the Tyne with coal and returned in ballast. Sand ballast was sometimes used to supply local industries, like the Tyneside glassworks, but often it was shovelled out of the

hold and dumped overboard. For hundreds of years seamen had been fined for illegally dumping ballast: as early as 1655 there were complaints that the Tyne was silting up (Gardiner). By 1765 the river had 'so deteriorated through neglect and the dropping overboard of ballast that where ships used to load and lie afloat at low water was then dry in several places' (Hodgson).

By the mid-1850s there were over 30 screw-driven iron colliers with double-bottom tanks exporting coals from Newcastle: solid ballast was soon to be a thing of the past. But the legacy was still there; the Tyne was a shallow river and needed to be deepened if it was to be turned into a 'great highway of commerce'. The Victorians set to work with their usual energy. In 1850 Newcastle was finally forced to relinquish some of its power over the river when Parliament passed the Tyne Navigation Act, which decided that total control of the river was finally to be taken from Newcastle and given to a Tyne Improvement Commission. The commission was made up of 18 members: two from Gateshead, three from both North and South Shields, six from the Newcastle Corporation and four from the Admiralty.

The commission's first act was to build two massive piers at the river mouth, to make the entrance safer and increase flow rate to scour and deepen the channel. Work started in 1854 and, after numerous failures due to wall breaches by severe gales, the piers were finally completed in 1895.

To improve the main Tyne the commissioners' engineer, J. F. Ure, believed in using the new steam-powered dredgers. Dredging transformed the lower reaches into 'a busy waterway deep enough to take ocean steamers up to Newcastle Quay and to float warships from the Elswick shipyard. Whitehall Point and Bill Point were cut

away bodily, and away up at Lemington the channel was straightened so that the tidal flow was carried inland to Hedwin Streams.' In addition, 'the Northumberland Dock, Tyne Dock and Albert Edward Dock were constructed, the old Tyne bridge at Newcastle demolished and replaced by the graceful swing bridge and later Dunston Staithes, east and west, erected. The never-ceasing work of the dredger has scooped 160 million tons of material from the bottom of the river and carried it out to sea.' (Johnson, 1934.)

The Northumberland Dock was built for the coal mines north of the river, while the Tyne Dock and Dunston Staithes served those to the south. The Tyne Dock exported more coal than any other dock in the world and could simultaneously load more than 16 colliers from its four staithes and 42 spouts. But the increase in shipping also brought problems: ships were thought by many to increase pollution in the estuary. Following an outbreak of cholera on the Continent, the Newcastle Medical Officer of Health suggested in 1892 that vessels should not discharge their freshwater ballast and bilge water into the Tyne, but rather into the open sea. For centuries drinking water had come from the Tyne but in the early nineteenth century several outbreaks of cholera had occurred on Tyneside, the worst in 1853. It was then decided to stop taking drinking water from the Tyne and use only the local wells, streams and reservoirs which had

Heavy weather. The piers at the mouth of the Tyne c. 1900.

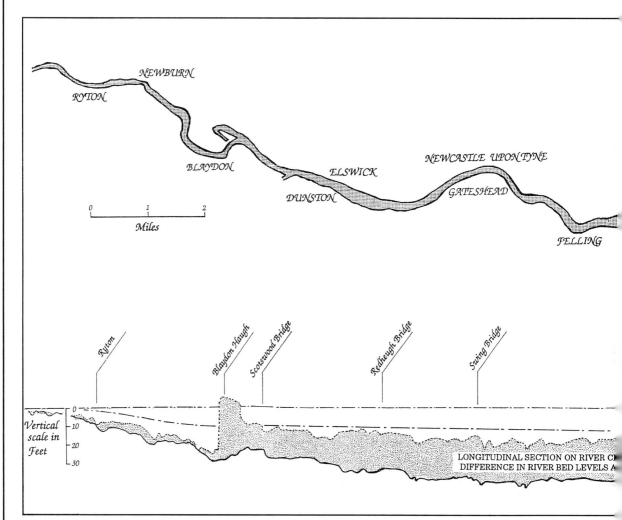

Vertical scale in feet

0
10
20
30

LONGITUDINAL SECTION ON RIVER C[...]
DIFFERENCE IN RIVER BED LEVELS A[...]

been alternative sources of water since the seventeenth century.

The unleashing of Victorian industrialism on the banks of the river caused a huge increase in the population of Tyneside. Not only was there more industrial effluent, there was also much more sewage. In the mid-nineteenth century both raw sewage and industrial waste were dumped untreated into the Tyne, and by the end of the century pollution levels began to increase dramatically. The deepening of the river was to have an adverse effect on the cleansing action of the tides. It was estimated that raw sewage lingered for up to ten days and, even worse, the sewage was pushed upstream by the incoming tides and began to settle on the river bed.

Still, in the mid- and late nineteenth century salmon were returning to the river and the salmon fisheries continued to function. But there was concern that 'the supply of salmon in the River Tyne, which was formerly most abundant, has greatly decreased, and there is reason to

The dredged lower Tyne, c. 1888.

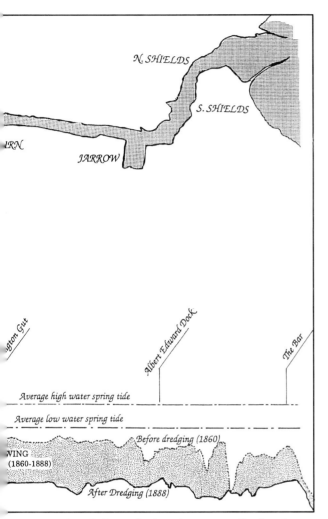

apprehend that a further decrease will take place, unless effectual measures be taken'. The measures resulted in an 'Act for Regulating and Maintaining the Fisheries in the River Tyne' that received royal assent in 1842. It banned the taking of fish from 10 September to 10 February, while during the open season fishing was forbidden after ten o'clock on Saturday night until two o'clock on Monday morning. It was made an offence for a salmon netsman to fish outside 'the land boundary of his fishery', a fine

between £1 and £10 was to be imposed for taking fish in the close season, spawning fish and 'salmon fry' were protected, and net mesh sizes were controlled. In 1851 all the fisheries in the Tyne were listed, eight of them being between the mouth of the river and Stannersford. The most expensive annual rent in this region was £100 charged by the Duke of Northumberland to Robert Forster for the Newburn Crumbwells fishery. The cheapest rent was £2 a year, charged to Henry Scott for the Heddon, Bounder Stone fishery.

By mid-nineteenth century, however, and generally throughout England and Wales, river salmon fisheries were yielding diminishing catches. Parliament passed a Salmon Fishery Act in 1861 for the 'purpose of increasing the supply of salmon'. The Act banned all 'fixed engines' for catching salmon in any inland or tidal waters, classifying any net that was 'temporarily fixed to the soil' as a fixed engine. Existing or newly constructed fishing weirs or fishing-mill dams had to have salmon passes, and the close season for catching salmon was from 1 September until 1 February for netsmen not using fixed engines, and from 1 November to 1 February for salmon anglers. Other Acts were passed between 1861 and 1865, and on 15 December 1866 the Board of Conservators for the Tyne Salmon Fishery District met for the first time at Hexham, in the Manor Office. The board was to be involved in taking proceedings 'against any person or persons acting in contravention of the Salmon Fishery Acts 1861–1865'. It also granted licences for the use of 'rod and line for fishing for salmon within the Tyne Salmon Fishery district' on the payment of the sum of £1. Salmon fishing licences were also issued for the use of draught or hang nets outside the 'Pier of Tynemouth' for a fee of £2, while it cost £5 to fish the Tyne with similar nets. A coracle net licence cost £2, the fee was £10 for each 'box, crib or cruive' (fishing traps), and funnel-shaped wickerwork traps, known as 'putts and putchers', were 2s. 6d. each and £1 for fifty respectively. The fee was £1 for every additional fifty putchers, 'or part thereof'. The board also received sums from 'persons entitled, for the time being, the exclusive right of fishing for salmon'. The rate was, for example, 'one farthing per running yard of river bank, on each side', for any person entitled to fish between Falstone Bridge and Kielder. The same amount was paid for each running yard for the stretches of river bank between Reedsmouth and Falstone Bridge, between Reedsmouth and West Woodburn Bridge, and from Warden Paper Mill to Bardon Mill. The cost dropped to one farthing per two running yards between West Woodburn Bridge and Elishaw Bridge, and dropped further to one farthing per four running yards for the stretches between Elishaw Bridge and Reedshead, and between Bardon Mill and Tyne Head. It was one halfpenny per running yard between South Tyne junction and Warden Paper Mill, as it was between Bywell Bridge and Reedsmouth. The amount increased to twopence per running yard for the stretch on the main Tyne between King's Meadows and Bywell Bridge.

As a result of the 1861 Act, inspectors made annual reports to Parliament on the state of the salmon fisheries. In their first annual report, published in 1862, the inspectors noted that, despite the 1842 Act, 'the value of the Tyne as a salmon river has of late years much decreased . . . due to the rise of shipping and want of protection in the river and the Bywell dam obstruction'. They thought that 'salmon may be more readily affected by polluted water than trout, and, sickened by it, may turn away'. Augustus Grimble, champion of the late nineteenth-century salmon angler and foe of the net

fisherman, wrote that the 'sorry plight' (as far as the salmon were concerned) of the main river and its branches in 1860 was not due to the increase in Newcastle shipping and sewage but to the 'ravages of the many stake nets working on either side of the river mouth'. The 1861 Act classified these stake nets as 'fixed engines' and they were thus prohibited within four and a half miles of the mouth of the Tyne on either side. But this still left, from the river mouth to the dam at Bywell, 18 stations for draught nets that, said Grimble, were 'hard fished'. The Bywell fishing dam offered a serious barrier to returning salmon since they could only pass when the river was in flood. The owner of the dam was forced by the Act to install a fish pass, but there were problems in constructing it; and so the owner, who 'took a great interest in the Tyne fisheries, and being anxious that the owners above him should share in the benefits of the 1861 Act . . . very generously gave up his cruives, and in 1862 the dam was destroyed'. The effect was immediate and the Tyne became well stocked with fish which were caught in places and numbers that before were unknown; for example, 25 miles above Bellingham more than 25 salmon were taken with the rod in the 1862 season. The South Tyne still suffered from pollution from lead mines and paper mills and from the obstruction of Warden Weir, but heavy spates were experienced and after a good fish pass was made in 1867 at the Warden Dam the salmon continued to increase to such an extent that new spawning grounds had to be opened 'to accommodate their numbers'. By 1870 an important obstacle, the Woodburn Dam on the River Rede, the North Tyne's largest tributary, had been removed and 'bull trout' were appearing in the Rede for the first time. But pollution was intensifying. Furthermore, once in the river, salmon were constantly being poached both during and outside the close season; and the newly invented drift or hang nets were killing large numbers of fish at sea even before they reached fresh water.

Pollution from the lead mines around Alston in 1870 had made the South Tyne, which often had better runs of fish than the North Tyne, almost useless for salmon fishing. Smolts returning to the sea were killed as they tried to pass through the pollution barriers rapidly building up around Newcastle. To make matters worse the Newcastle and Gateshead Water Company began extracting water from the river, and 'nine-tenths of Hexham sewage' – a town of some 5000 people where there were 'comparatively few privies, water closets being in general use' – was run into the Tyne by one outfall. 'Perhaps something like 70,000 or 80,000 gallons may be the quantity flowing by this channel.' (Hexham Local Board of Health, 1869.) By 1887 there was pollution from 'collieries, lead mines, dye works, paper mills, tan yards, alkali and other chemical works and sewage . . . and it was feared that . . . the Tyne might eventually become as salmonless as the Bristol Avon, the Mersey, the Aire and Calder, the Weaver, the Taff, Ogmore and many smaller rivers from which salmon has been exterminated solely by poisonous pollutions' (Grimble). In 1882 Palmer wrote that 'apart from the visitation of its industries, few would care to linger by the banks of the Lower Tyne, or select as the route of a walking excursion the riverside countryside between Newcastle and the sea'.

Nevertheless, some excellent years for rod-caught salmon were had in the 1880s and 1890s. Heavy spates must have helped, and pollution was not yet bad enough to prevent smolt migration and inhibit the passage of returning salmon. There was, however, a very dry summer in 1895 which resulted in reduced flow rates

and increased pollution levels in the estuary – salmon smolts died in their thousands as they tried to negotiate the brackish waters of the main Tyne.

Throughout much of the 1800s salmon continued to fetch high prices and poaching was a worthwhile occupation. In 1834 the South Tyne, and the North Tyne and Redewater 'Associations for the Prevention of Poaching' were formed. A letter written to the associations from the Benwell fishery in 1834 argued that the 'manufactories have long been blamed for the decrease of salmon in the River Tyne but they . . . are not the cause – killing in close time is, if not the only cause, the most . . . one, and if that is checked, or in a great measure put a stop to, there is little doubt [that] of the River Tyne producing as many salmon as formerly' (Hopper). In 1862, the second annual report of the inspectors described the poachers as invariably the lowest and worst class of the community, and as such are known by the police, who are respected and feared by the poacher'.

The poachers often had great successes. In the pool that existed below the Bywell dam before it was removed, over 200 salmon were taken on one occasion during the close season. In 1863 the Chief Constable of Northumberland became involved in the attempts to control poaching by authorising patrols along the parts of the Tyne and North Tyne that were under his jurisdiction. The Tyne Fisheries Association undertook to pay the constables' expenses, each constable being paid a halfpenny per yard of river frontage of his beat.

There was severe poaching at the river mouth by both fixed, 'floating' and 'sunk' nets and it was not until the 1870s that steps were taken to try and reduce it. In 1875 the Tyne Salmon Fishery Board hired extra 'watchers' to try and stop poaching with 'sunk nets' along the coast near the river mouth. At that time a 'great deal of pilfering of fish from the nets of licensed fishermen was reported to be going on during the fishing season, by men who go out in small boats adapted for the purpose, and from whom it is impossible to defend themselves, as their heavy boats cannot be moved so rapidly through the water as those which the thieves use'. A Sergeant Harbottle was empowered by the board to use 'small boats or any other means he thinks most likely to put a stop to the practice'.

Poaching using a floating, hang or drift net was a particularly effective way of taking salmon. The drift nets first made their appearance in the sea off the River Tyne in 1867. The principle of the drift net is simple: the top is hung from corks, while the bottom is weighted with a leaded line so the net hangs vertically, like a curtain, in the water. The nets are shot, ideally across the tide, and the fishermen's boats lie head-on to the wind with their bows attached by a rope to the ends of the nets. Salmon are caught when they enter the net and their gills become entangled in the mesh.

When the nets were first legally used, their 'destructive powers were not fully understood, even by those who worked them'. The early drift nets were made from heavy hemp netting and, being hard to work, were left down for hours after being shot. The result was that fish caught in these nets were both 'drowned and hanged . . . they became sodden with water and very inferior food . . . in fact there is as much difference in eating a drift-net fish and a draught-net one as there is between eating a mutton that has been drowned and mutton that has been killed by a butcher' (Grimble).

The drift nets were legally used off the Tyne estuary by coastal fishermen from the fishing communities of Newbiggin, Blyth, Cullercoats,

North Shields and to some extent Sunderland. They drift-netted using an open boat that is unique to England's north-east coast – the coble. The coble is of ancient origin, perhaps evolving from the Viking longboat, but it is still used by the present-day drift netsmen. Over the centuries cobles were developed to be launched and retrieved on the gently shelving beaches that make up much of north-east England's coast. The coble is clinker-built, traditionally of larch planks on oak frames, and made strong enough to weather a North Sea gale or to land on a beach in heavily breaking surf. Cobles are difficult craft to work. The inshore fishermen in the 1880s, who used only sails and oars, believed that 'you must be born in a coble if you want to learn anything about her'. Most modern coble fishermen would probably agree, despite their boats being fitted with reliable diesel engines. From 1867 the drift netsmen fished for salmon only at night with their heavy hemp nets, as the mesh was easily seen by the salmon during the day. The best night-drifting was when the sea was rough and the bottom stirred – and then, 'the men that dared caught fish'. Then as now, son followed father to 'the fishing'. The young fisher-lad dressed in his first oilskins

> feels himself manly as he sits amidships while the coble skims out into the bay. He is usually sent to the trouting (salmon) first; and then all night long he glides about on the dark bay and hears sounds from the moor and the wood. It falls cold toward the dawn, and the boy grows hard and strong through his night ordeal. When his hands are properly hardened like his horny feet (the fisher-lads went everywhere bare-foot), he is allowed to row the coble with crossed oars; and then he becomes useful, for the men are left free to haul nets and plash on the water to frighten the trout.
> (Runciman, 1883.)

Grimble wrote that in 1870 'the ravages of 33 drift or hang nets working the mouth began to decrease the stock of fish, the sea nets taking 18,950 salmon and the river nets 17,500 salmon'. Drift netting was running out of control. By 1872 the nets were up to 1400 yards long and in that year took over 130,000 migratory fish; one 600-yard net took 120 salmon in two hours. In the following year some nets were two miles long and the fishermen had taken to anchoring them in place. In 1872 it was decided to ban all nets from the mouth of the Tyne to form a 'playground or sanctuary' for the returning salmon. This had some success, for the inspectors' report of 1878 stated that, 'The high level bridge at Newcastle upon Tyne crosses one of the most, if not the most, important of the English salmon rivers, namely the Tyne.'

There has always been tension between salmon anglers and legal commercial netsmen. Augustus Grimble, writing in the early 1900s, acknowledged it and, while 'hating the nets that kill alike both kelts and clean fish', he had many friends amongst the drift netsmen who fished off the Tyne. He recognised that they were poor and 'for the sake of the wives and bairns they must keep the wolf from the door'. Grimble believed that the netsmen were a 'brave, hardy, honest, hard-working, law-abiding lot of stalwart men' but nevertheless was for making the Tyne estuary 'playground' larger and the net season two weeks shorter. This would, he argued, at first cause some hardship amongst the coble fishermen, but they would later reap the benefits and catch 'more fish and better ones'.

Drift netting continued, however, and in 1891 it was estimated that there were 25 miles of drift nets working an area off the river mouth that was just 25 miles long. The salmon runs had to suffer. In 1901, the year Queen Victoria died, there were 65 drift-net licences issued to the coble fishermen. This number increased to 78 in 1927, but fell to 63 in 1930 and to 24 in 1945. Some coastal fishing communities, like Cullercoats, died. Others, like Newbiggin, survive today. The drift nets off the river mouth and the nets in the Tyne continued to catch some very large salmon. One of 52 lb. was caught off Briar Dene in July 1880, and another of 47½ lb. was taken off Seaton Sluice on 7 August 1913. In the river the Scotswood fishery caught a fish of 48⅓ lb. in June 1873, while in August 1903 the Stella fishery had a 46 lb. salmon as did the Benwell Boat House on 14 June 1912 (Bolam).

In 1891 there were between 40 and 50 fishing stations working draft (or draught) nets from the banks of the Tyne, but their numbers too began to fall. There were peaks in the early 1930s after the tremendous salmon runs of 1927 and 1928, but by 1934 net fishing for salmon in the Tyne was over. It was the end of a tradition that was at least a thousand, perhaps two thousand years old.

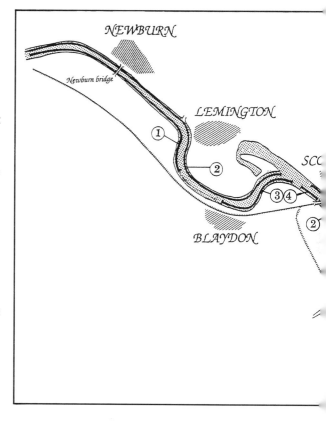

One of the last of the river netsmen is Walter Stokoe. Walter's father Robert, his elder brother Jimmy, his grandfather (also Robert) and his great-grandfather were all salmon fishermen. At least four generations of Stokoes have swept draft nets through the Tyne every spring and summer. In winter the Stokoes made new nets, mended old ones and repaired their boat. When they could, they odd-jobbed. It was an uncertain business. Walter Stokoe recalls: 'In the mid to late twenties we were beginning to get complaints from the fishmongers about the salmon; they were starting to taste bad and that was a shame, because in 1928 we had one of our best seasons ever, there were thousands of fish in the river. By the thirties the river stank, like dead bodies. In 1934 it was

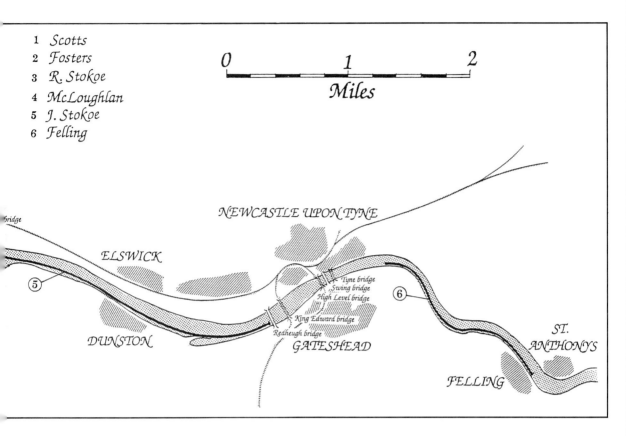

1 *Scotts*
2 *Fosters*
3 *R. Stokoe*
4 *McLoughlan*
5 *J. Stokoe*
6 *Felling*

all over, the salmon fishing died.'

Walter Stokoe was born in 1909 at Wallace Cottages, Ryton, and at four years of age was down at the river's edge watching his father and grandfather at work. His father Robert was born at Stella in 1871 and died at Wallace Cottages in 1934, and for most of his life, like his father and grandfather, worked the Blaydon fishery. In Robert's time the Tyne was a much shallower river than it is today, running through rocks, sandbanks and shingle, even turning 'back on itself' on the north side at Lemington Point. If the tide was out it could be easily waded; Robert Stokoe used to roll up his trousers and 'plodge' across the river at Lemington on his way to the Saturday dance. The salmon netsmen relied

heavily on spates to bring fish up the river to Blaydon. Spates were more common before the development of a 'managed Tyne' and the Kielder Reservoir: heavy rain on the high Northumbrian fells would swell the small burns and tributaries flowing into the main river, and the water level would rise rapidly. Salmon would congregate in the sea off the river entrance, forming large shoals, and it was common to see them leaping as if impatient for a good spate, waiting to be off on their upstream run to the spawning grounds at the first hint of a flood. In Walter's time, a good spring or summer spate was when the river at Blaydon rose by five, six, or even more feet; then Robert Stokoe would tell his son that within 36 hours they were going to have salmon in the Blaydon nets.

The lower Tyne salmon fisheries, after W. Stokoe, c. 1920.

But sudden spates were dangerous. Walter Stokoe recalls one Sunday morning when he and his brother, and the rest of the netsmen, had fished their way upstream from Blaydon to the west side of Newburn Bridge and were approaching the old Ryton ferry, which was on the north bank of the river about 100 yards to the west of today's ferry house. The fishermen often moored their boats at Ryton ferry and were approaching their mooring buoy when suddenly they were hit by a heavy spate – a flash flood. Within minutes the water level had risen by some ten feet, and they were forced downstream in the grip of a powerful current. Easing the boat as near as they dared to the bank, Walter's brother Jimmy leapt ashore with a bow rope but the current was too powerful: he could not hold the boat. The situation was only saved by 'Big Jack' Wealans, who by rowing with all his force was able to hold the bow's head to the current. Without his skill and strength the Blaydon netsmen would have been swept away, their boat rolled over, and the men perhaps entangled in the heavy salmon net when it slid off the stern.

There was friendly rivalry between the men of the different salmon fisheries; they were all good

At the Scotswood Fishery, c. 1920. Bob Foster is to the right, wearing the bowler hat.

friends, but usually the men from each fishery stayed together. Anyone could obtain a salmon fishery providing he could afford the nets and 'ground rents', but in practice the fisheries usually stayed within a few families who passed fishing skills and river knowledge down through the generations. To gain extra money, the salmon fishermen sometimes worked as ferrymen. Three Scott brothers – Archie, George and Joss – had the Ryton fishery, and Joss Scott worked the Ryton ferry. Walter's father also rowed the boat at the Ryton ferry in Joss's absence. In the early 1900s they charged a penny a crossing for adults, a halfpenny for children.

The Stokoe family had two salmon fisheries, so Walter Stokoe had the choice of working either with his elder brother Jimmy (born in 1906), who had a fishery at Newcastle, or with his father at Blaydon. Walter Stokoe recalls that the lowest salmon fishery was from Felling to 200 yards upstream of Bill Quay. His brother had the next station from above Redheugh Bridge to the old Scotswood suspension bridge. The next station was worked by the Fosters, who netted up-river from the Scotswood suspension bridge to the east side of Scotswood railway bridge. The next belonged to the McLoughlans. Then Robert Stokoe had the Blaydon fishery which ended some 200 yards upstream of Blaydon railway station near the ferry that went across the Tyne from Blaydon to Newburn Haugh. The Scott brothers had the next stretch, opposite Spencer's works, that ended near Ryton Willows station. On the north side of the river 'Dutcher' Foster had the fishery from the 'old steps' (half-way along Ryton Willows) to Lemington Point. This was not a very good fishery as there were only a few places where nets could be landed; one was opposite Stella Staithes below the Stella North power station. To make matters worse, the Duke of

Northumberland, who owned the land from Wylam Bridge to Lemington Point, except for the Close House section, claimed a shilling off Dutcher Foster for every salmon he landed. 'That was a lot of money in those days, and you can imagine that the salmon were not always declared!' said Walter Stokoe. The Wallaces had a fishery for about 100 yards above Wylam Bridge and the use of the waters in front of Close House at Wylam. There were also fisheries at Ovingham and Mickley.

The salmon netsmen negotiated their 'ground rents', which might be as much as £5 a season and entitled them to land their nets on different stretches of the river bank, with the local landowners. The netsmen were often successful in 'bumming a tale' to a landowner, arguing that his section of the river bank was very difficult to fish owing to rocky overhangs, underwater obstructions and tree roots and as a result the ground rent should be reduced. The netsmen's season opened on 22 February and lasted until 31 August. Fishing began at six every Monday morning and finished at noon on Saturday so as to give the salmon a chance to pass through the netting stations. Robert Stokoe always said he would have swapped the first two months of the season for an extra one at the 'back end'. In 1924 a local by-law was passed preventing the fishermen from taking their nets the full width of the river; half the river was to be left clear for the passage of salmon. A bailiff spotted Robert Stokoe and the Blaydon fishermen taking their nets two-thirds of the way across. In court Robert Stokoe's honest defence that he had fished the river all his life and had never heard of the by-law was not accepted. The magistrate fined the Blaydon Salmon Fishery £50, half to be paid by Robert Stokoe, the rest to be paid by the other netsmen.

In general, at each fishery four or five men

worked a draft (sweep) net using the shot-wear technique. The net hung down from a top rope that, in the Stokoe nets, was kept afloat by corks spaced about a yard apart. The bottom of the net was attached to the ground rope which was often weighted with lead strips. The net was carefully loaded on to boards nailed across the back of the fishermen's heavy clinker-built boat; then with one end of the net held ashore, and with the current flowing downstream and the salmon swimming upstream, the boat was rowed off, first across the river and then down, the net streaming off the boards in the stern as the boat made way through the water. The men ashore kept pace with the boat as it was rowed downstream and back towards the shore, the net forming a half-circle with the middle section trapping fish in the 'pocket'. The middle or 'bag' section was buoyed up by five corks, and the ends of the bag were marked with white-painted corks so that it could

be easily identified. The bag section was pulled ashore carefully and evenly: two corks on each side, one in the middle. The Blaydon fishermen used different nets according to the conditions: deep nets for a river in flood, which were up to 60 yards long and had a mesh of either six or seven inches depending on the time of year. The front or 'fore-part' of the net was often attached to a wooden stake which kept the top and ground ropes apart. Once the net was all out a rope from the fore-part was passed ashore from the boat to the 'fore-hand' who, if the station was lucky enough, attached it to a horse. Lacking a horse the men had to haul in by hand. The fore-hand and 'upper-hands' heaved on the top rope, the other men on the ground rope, with as many as ten sweeps an hour. Pulling in up to 60 yards of heavy hemp net at every sweep was back-breaking work, especially for the men on the ground rope who were bent double keeping it as close to the

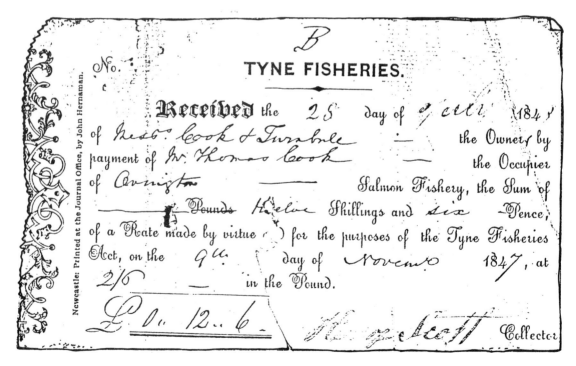

Ovington Salmon Fishery licence, dated 1847.

river bottom as possible to prevent any fish escaping underneath.

Salmon fishing often paid well. In the 1920s engineering apprentices on Tyneside were earning about 7s. 6d. for a five-and-a-half-day week. Then salmon could fetch as much as 1s. 1d. a pound (up to 1s. 9d. in exceptional times), and most Tyne salmon caught in the sweep nets weighed between 10 and 12 lb. Walter Stokoe's largest single haul was 29 fish – salmon, sea trout and grilse – and catches of 50 migratory fish a day were not uncommon. His biggest salmon was a 43-pounder and in the same haul there were two 30-lb. fish that, according to Walter, 'looked like sardines!' As a young man Walter Stokoe earned more money than many of his friends, but in 1930, when the river died, he followed them to work full time down the local pit.

Walter Stokoe recalls his fishing days with great affection. 'They were happy times, we were drawn to the river; as bairns we swam in it; we fought in it; ate picnics by it and as adults we fished it. I remember once as a boy having to take my father's breakfast down to him. It was early on a Monday morning, he had been down on the river since four, soaking the nets so they would sink and be ready for the six o'clock start. It was a moment I shall never forget.' Walter Stokoe describes how he ran down the river bank, below Blaydon station, too frightened to take the short cut through the dark woods of the Dene and, in the full joy of his childhood, splashed across the river. He looked downstream. It was a beautiful morning, beams of sunlight were breaking through the overnight mist that lay over a foot deep on the water. The mist was slowly lifting as a single hazy cloud, burnt off by a sun that promised a long hot summer's day. The glides close to the steep banks were still dark in the long morning shadows. They flowed deep and

mysterious, but bright and sparkling were the shallow, midstream runs that caught and reflected the early sunlight. He looked downstream and saw salmon leaping, glinting silver, disappearing into the mist to reappear and hit the water with a 'plop' that he could hear above the noise of his splashing feet. Time froze. 'It was the bonniest sight of my life. I'll never forget it.'

Robert, Jimmy and Walter Stokoe knew every salmon hole and pool from Wylam to Newcastle. In the hot summer months, when spates were few and far between and salmon scarce, then, at the Blaydon fishery, Robert and Walter would sweep for single fish. The netsmen would lie in wait on the top of the river bank, searching the runs and pools for the tell-tale V of a returning salmon. Once one was sighted they would carefully slide off the bank to carry their nets to the pool. Cautiously rowing out their nets, they made a single sweep and nearly always caught the fish.

Salmon were often scarce at Easter, when they were always in great demand and fetched a high price. One Easter, the Blaydon netsmen had been fishing since first light, ranging up and down the river looking for fish. (It was agreed amongst the netsmen that boats could fish any fishery, provided that it was not being worked by the regular netsmen.) By early morning they had only five fish: three salmon fresh in from the sea, and two kelts, females that after breeding were on their way back to the sea. By law the netsmen should have returned the kelts to the river, but money and fish were scarce and the kelts were well mended. All five salmon were boxed up and rowed over to the Ryton Willows railway station ready to catch the six o'clock Newcastle train, due in a few minutes, to be taken to Central Station where they would be collected by Mr Vies, a Newcastle fishmonger. Half-way across the river they heard a cry of 'Boat, boat', and on looking downstream they could see Mr Crawford, the bailiff, coming down from the high side of Newburn Bridge where he lived.

'Don't fetch him over until they're on the train,' said Robert Stokoe.

Arriving on time, the Newcastle train pulled out of the station with its box of five salmon safely in the guard's van. Robert Stokoe returned to the river and was in time to overhear the bailiff say to the netsmen, 'Where's Robert? I know he's got two kelts in the box.'

'Hello, Mr Crawford,' said Robert Stokoe, suddenly appearing.

'Where are the kelts?' demanded the bailiff.

'I've fished all my life, and if I don't know the difference between a fresh salmon and a kelt I'll eat my horse.'

'Don't bum the tale with me,' said the bailiff. 'Where are they?'

'At Mr Vies's, the fishmonger's, Newcastle,' capitulated Robert.

The bailiff took the next train to Newcastle, tracked down the fishmonger and confiscated the kelts. It was the Easter holidays, so it was not until five days later that the Blaydon netsmen appeared in court. The bailiff, holding up the two kelts, one in each hand, argued that he thought Robert Stokoe should be heavily fined for knowingly taking 'unclean fish'.

'But those fish look like two lovely specimens to me,' said the magistrate.

The bailiff, slightly exasperated, explained to the court that they were kelts and unclean.

'But why call them unclean? They look healthy to me,' continued the magistrate, not convinced.

The bailiff patiently explained that the salmon had just spawned and had to return to the sea to make themselves clean. At this point the magistrate interrupted and asked Robert Stokoe if he had anything to say about clean fish.

The shallow, Tyne, c. 1875. Probably Scotswood.

'Yes sir,' Robert replied. 'If you had been lying on ice in a wooden coffin for five days, wouldn't you come out unclean?' The magistrate agreed, and this time Robert Stokoe and his colleagues were acquitted.

Towards the end of the nineteenth century there was still hope for the returning salmon. In 1876 an exclusive Newcastle angling club had been formed 'for gentlemen'. 'The season of 1891, so far as regards the yield of Salmon, may be considered, very satisfactory.' (McAllum, 1891.) In 1908 there was 'no doubt about the salmon in the North Tyne . . . the salmon fishing is everywhere excellent' (Bradley). The Tyne River Police helped the returning salmon by catching poachers and preventing river pollution. An entry made on 10 October 1910 in the River Police charge book reveals that 'John Stoker Brown and James Ripley, both of South Shields, had in their possession an unseasonable salmon not having obtained the same for artificial propagation or other scientific purposes' [*sic*]. They were fined 50s. and 40s. respectively after being charged by Thomas Dagg, Inspector of Fisheries for the Tyne Conservancy Board. In 1913 George Stoddart was charged with 'unlawfully being in possession of a salmon gaff for the purpose of taking salmon from the River Tyne'. He was fined 10s. with costs. There are many such entries in the charge book as well as others concerned with illegal dumping. Such an entry was made in 1907 when Frank Larcomba, a boy on board the schooner *Queen of Clippers*, was charged with 'unlawfully casting a quantity of ashes into the River Tyne, within the port, contrary to the Tyne Improvement Act of 1857'. Another entry, dated 1913, notes that a member of the crew of the steam wherry *Lily* was fined for being drunk and disorderly and 'casting refuse in the river'.

On previous pages: *The smoke and grime on Tyneside, at Pipewell Quay, off Bridge Street, Gateshead, c. 1886. Two small boys search the clinker-built boat in the foreground.*

By 1930, however, serious damage had been done to the salmon fishing. As the chairman of the Tyne Improvement Commission wrote in 1927,

> *The development of Tyneside was rapid. Quays and staithes took the place of green fields and pleasant woods. Islands were removed and projecting points cut off. Ship-yards, dry-docks, wet-docks, factories and arsenals destroyed the salmon fishery, but created in its stead industries that employ a ¼ million people and supply the world with ships, guns, steel-rails and coal . . .*

Trouble came not only from the shipyards and other works. Throughout the nineteenth and early twentieth centuries Tyneside's population had been growing at an unprecedented rate. It was the raw sewage dumped into the lower reaches of the Tyne by the expanding population that, more than anything, was responsible for ending the salmon runs. In 1800 Newcastle had some 15,000 inhabitants; the other ancient towns on Tyneside – Gateshead, South Shields, North Shields – each had around 8000. Tynemouth had some 4000, Wallsend 1000 and Jarrow less than 1000. There were other smaller towns and villages, and when all were added together they gave a total Tyneside population of around 80,000. By 1921 this total had increased to 800,000. Towns and villages along the river banks were merging. Scotswood, once a village, became part of Newcastle and in 1928 was described as consisting of 'rows of dismal houses'. Although the Tyne was pleasant enough just above Blaydon, 'below that point it loses its ripple and is badly polluted'. (Mess quoted by Rennison.) Thousands of gallons of untreated sewage flowed into the tidal Tyne. It became an example of that all-too-common twentieth-century phenomenon: the grossly polluted estuary.

The meeting of the North and South Tyne.

I have picked up a few stories in my rambles that I am sure will interest you at the season. First of all, let me tell you that of the King of Fishes. I suppose you guess that I mean the salmon. Like so many true stories it is a wonderful one. If you saw a big salmon, a forty pounder say, ready to be cut up and eaten, you would never guess that such a monster was once a teeny-weeny egg laid with hundreds of others in the gravelly bottom of a river by old Mrs Salmon. You might know this to be the case if you had been told, but you could never imagine it without. The eggs are laid in the autumn. They hatch out in about a 100 days, and the wee little fishes swim about in the water as lively as grigs – not salmon yet any more than a tadpole is a frog, but going to be by and by. Their sides are marked by dark bands now, and naturalists and fishers call them parr. Can you remember this? People used to be puzzled about this very thing, but now we know for true that parr are salmon in their infancy.

Next a funny thing happens, the salmon that is going to be puts off its parrdress, and comes out in a new one. After this change it is no longer a parr, but a smolt. When it gets its smolt-dress on, it is getting a grown-up fish, not quite, but nearly. It does not have to stay in the nursery of the river any longer, but goes off to sea. This trip to the sea does wonders, and brings about another change. When they come back again to the river they are grilse, or young salmon, about 4 or 5 lbs in weight. Some people say they always come back to the very same river in which they were hatched. They can lay eggs themselves now, so they set to work and do this, and then off to the sea again. When next they come back to the river they are salmon. Now can you remember all their changes? First an egg, then parr, then smolt, then grilse, and last of all salmon. Is not that an interesting story?

Hexham Courant, 9 August 1890

Chapter 3

A Managed, Cleaner, Salmon River

'We would wait until they were nicely settled, and then quietly open the hatch that led out on to the back-lane. We had a five-foot-long bamboo pole, with a candle stuck on the end. We'd wait for the shout before we ran,' said James Cheeseman, an eighty-year-old Tynesider, describing a childhood prank played on the occupant of a 'midden', 'netty' or 'earth closet'. Middens were found in the backyards of thousands of Tyneside houses at the beginning of the twentieth century, one closet often serving up to four families. A well-scrubbed wooden plank with a hole acted as both the seat and the hinged lid of the wooden 'thunder-box'. The box was built against the closet's rear wall, which contained the street-level hatch. The closet was usually lit with a candle carried by the user, and candle-soot marks can still be seen on the walls of backyard buildings that once acted as middens. Ashes from the house's coal fires were stored in buckets and poured through the hole in the lid when required. 'It was always nice to sit in the closet on a cold winter's day with warm ashes inside the box, but this was the time for another prank,' said Mr Cheeseman. A cat was introduced into the wooden box through the hatch in the wall. Once it made contact with the warm ashes, the cat's only thought was escape. The sole exit was the gap between the occupant's legs – the cat's claws left large scratch marks if the ashes

were very hot and the occupier unlucky.

Street-level hatches can still be seen at the rear of some pre-1914 Tyneside houses, where the night-soil men, or 'midnight mechanics' as they were sometimes called, regularly removed the soil from the wooden toilets with their flat-bladed shovels. The hatches were never locked, but were usually closed with a bent nail that could be easily swung by the night-soil men – and also the children! The soil was carried away on horse-drawn carts, and often stored in yards or cesspits before being distributed to nearby farms and market gardens for fertiliser. But some was just dumped into disused quarries and pits, and some found its way into the Tyne. In South Shields, night soil was tipped off Lawe Top straight into the river. 'Since time immemorial the Tyne has acted as the receptacle for most of the waste generated on the river banks.' (TJSB.)

In medieval Newcastle, sewage ran down channels cut into the middle of the narrow streets, and was piled along the road. These piles were also known as middens. People were used to the sight and smell of raw sewage. Because of the general lack of public transport, nineteenth-century Tyneside industrial workers were crammed into hovels near their workplaces, and the everyday smell in these slums must have been terrible. Dozens of families were served by a single water pump – people rarely washed after working long hours. In 1842 a report on Gateshead housing complained that 'each small, ill ventilated apartment of the house contained a family with the lodgers in numbers from seven to nine, and seldom more than two beds for the whole. The want of convenient offices induces the lazy inmates to make use of chamber utensils . . . which remain in the most offensive state for several days and are then emptied out of the window.' (*Chadwick Report*, 1842, quoted in

Rennison.) Only after 1845 was there any real concept of public health and 'sanitation', and only towards the end of the nineteenth century was government legislation introduced to improve health and reduce water pollution. Two Acts were passed: the Public Health Act of 1875 and the Rivers Pollution Prevention Act of 1876.

By the twentieth century other industries had proliferated on the banks of the Tyne: gas, coke, tar, steel and chemical works, coal-fired electricity generating stations and metal-plating shops. All discharged industrial effluent into the Tyne, but if industrial effluent had been the only pollutant salmon might still have returned throughout the century.

In 1912 a water sample taken at Newcastle quay recorded zero oxygen content. The main cause of river deoxygenation is organic pollution. Dissolved oxygen is used by water-borne bacteria to break down, i.e. purify or oxidise, organic material. The greater the organic pollution the greater the oxygen loss, and if dissolved oxygen levels fall much below 30 per cent of saturation, salmon and sea trout are unable to survive. In 1912 the deoxygenated Tyne estuary was not only a serious barrier to any returning salmon, but prevented any smolts migrating to the sea.

The main organic pollutant in the Tyne during the twentieth century was sewage, and one of the main polluters was the water closet. It was common on Tyneside by the 1920s and at first caused much pollution, since 'it was wrongly felt by some that as the WCs caused more dilution of the sewage, it would lessen the problem rather than accentuate it' (TJSB). The rich on Tyneside had been served by water closets and sewers since the 1820s, but it was not until the late nineteenth century that they were more widely introduced. By 1896 there were some 29,000 WCs in use compared to 8000 privy pans and ashpits

(Rennison). The earliest Tyneside council estates were built after the First World War, and in the mid-1920s an intensive house-reconditioning programme was started. In the 1930s there was a rapid increase in the number of private estates, and after the Second World War the number of council estates was rapidly expanded. All these new houses had flushing toilets, and raw sewage and domestic water waste went straight into the river.

'Once you fall in the Tyne you're as good as dead. Even if you don't drown, one mouthful of water will cut your lifespan in half,' said a foyboatman describing the state of the river before the clean-up began (TJSB). Foyboatmen have worked and been intimately connected with the River Tyne for hundreds of years. In the days of sail, when there were light or contrary winds, narrow-beamed foyboats towed the colliers in and out of the river. The foyboatmen also assisted in 'kedge-hauling' the ships out to sea against strong winds and tides. The foyboatmen rowed out the ship's kedge anchor so that the crew could haul the collier up to the anchor – a process that was repeated again and again to obtain precious distance. Towing and kedging were carried out under oars: laborious, back-breaking jobs that disappeared when steam power replaced sail, and tugs took over. But foyboatmen still worked the Tyne, mooring ships to the river's many staithes, buoys, docks and quays. In the 1920s and 1930s there were some 200 licensed foyboatmen handling, day and night, the heavy mooring ropes and wires of over 15,000 ships each year. Oil from these ships and their other discharges all added to the general river pollution. The foyboatmen not only needed to be tough, they had to have strong stomachs. For underneath their boats flowed the noxious Tyne, deep and oily, sometimes green and bubbling with gas from decaying waste. The river often smelt of rotten eggs, an indicator of hydrogen sulphide gas – the gas of putrefaction.

A Ministry of Agriculture, Fisheries and Food (MAFF) committee that sat between 1922 and 1931, obtaining evidence on Tyne pollution, finally produced a report that declared the river to be 'nauseating and thoroughly objectionable' near sewer outfalls, and that during the summer months there was serious deoxygenation of the river between Ryton and Wallsend. In 1935 there were 180 major sewage outfalls from Ryton down to the sea, and the smell from the river was intolerable. A Tyne Sewerage Committee was created and in 1936 produced a report. After first noting that 'every person immersed involuntarily in the river contracted septic pneumonia', it stated that

> the pollution is due to the fact that the sewage of 800,000 people, in an area almost entirely provided with water closets, is discharged into the tidal portion of the river without any treatment and at all states of the tide. In addition, noxious liquids are discharged from a large number of works with, in the majority of instances, no prior treatment . . . the concentration and semi-stagnation of polluting matter make the upper portion of the estuary virtually into a septic tank.

But the Tyne Sewerage Committee did nothing as the Second World War interfered and a proposed scheme was dropped. After the war the Sewerage Committee re-formed, but again did nothing. The salmon anglers were the only body crying out for a clean river – over 15 miles of the Tyne had such a low oxygen content that fish could not survive. In 1947 the British Field Sport Society published a booklet on Tyne pollution and reported that 'At the present time Newcastle and Gateshead and the large towns down to the river mouth empty into the tidal reaches no less than 30 million gallons of entirely untreated sewage per day, or 10,950 million gallons per year.' It also recorded that well over 6000 million gallons of water were extracted from the Tyne and Rede in 1945, and that extraction 'has steadily increased since the Newcastle & Gateshead Water Company constructed the large reservoir at Catcleugh on the River Rede, a tributary to the North Tyne in 1904 . . . Through this increased extraction of fresh water, the polluted water in the estuary has not only increased in density but become more deadly to everyone, fish included.' The report also noted that proceedings against polluters 'cannot be taken under the Rivers Pollution Prevention Act, 1876, because the tidal water has not been declared "a stream", while the Fishery Board is practically powerless since it would be impossible to prove to the satisfaction of a Court of Law that any particular "death of fish" or similar claim under section 8 of the Salmon and Freshwater Fisheries Act had been caused by any one pollution'. The report suggested that main trunk sewers should be constructed to carry the waste to a purification works lower down the river, and that the effluent of this works should be taken to the sea.

By 1959 the Tyne was possibly the worst-polluted river in Britain, and was a serious health problem. In the 1958 annual report for the Northumbrian and Tyneside River Board J. L. Coxon, Medical Officer of Health to the Tyne Port Health Authority, wrote: 'Tyne water in the industrial belt has none of the accepted characteristics and quality of normal river water. It is lethal to fish, and to humans is probably more dangerous when swallowed than when inhaled.'

In 1959 the salmon rod returns were nil. Tyne anglers were in despair. The Northumbrian Anglers' Federation *Handbook and Guide* for 1960

described the river as 'an open ditch flowing through the middle of one of the greatest concentrations of population in this overcrowded island'. In 1959, along a 20-mile stretch of the main Tyne from Wylam to the sea, it was estimated that each day 270 sewers poured 35 million gallons of untreated sewage into the river.

Throughout the 1950s and 1960s, the Northumbrian Anglers' Federation fought hard to bring pressure on the government for money to clean up the river, but with little success. That the Tyne was dead as a fishing river was not considered to be important. The *Handbook and Guide* quoted a then familiar point of view: 'Why, many people will ask, should millions of pounds be spent to aid the sport of a comparatively few anglers? Let them fish on rivers that are cleaner.' The guide continued: 'This is undeniably logical from the view of the anti-clean-up brigade, and they are aided in their campaign by the fact that the most vocal groups in favour of cleaning up the Tyne are the anglers.'

In 1958, 14 Tyneside authorities joined together to try and solve the pollution problem. They were joined by six other local authorities, and these 20 authorities formed a Sewerage Board whose aim would be to 'examine the present and projected schemes for sewage disposal and to explore the possible ways of creating for the area a modern system of sewage disposal'. The board's long-term objective was to create conditions in the estuary which would support the passage of migratory fish at all states of the tide. In 1966 a Tyneside Joint Sewerage Board was set up to help bring about the construction of an effective sewage scheme. But progress was slow. In 1969 a public inquiry held on a hot summer's day in the Northumbrian Moot Hall at Newcastle, a short distance from the Tyne, had to be stopped because of the smell from the river.

Finally the Tyneside Sewage Treatment Scheme was developed: it was to be the biggest estuarial clean-up in Britain. Work started on the project in 1973, and in 1974 the Northumbrian Water Authority took over the project. The Northumbrian Water Authority was one of ten newly created authorities that were each regionally responsible for river management, water supply, sewerage and sewage disposal. The new authorities replaced those that had been previously created under the 1963 Water Resources Act. These authorities had themselves replaced the 34 river boards set up in 1948 for the control of land drainage, fisheries and pollution in England and Wales. In 1989 the water authorities were privatised. The National Rivers Authority was formed, with ten regions; the Northumbria Region is now responsible for the Tyne, for the river's flood defences, for protecting and improving fish stocks, and further conservation.

The Tyneside Sewage Treatment scheme was designed to clean up 20 miles of estuary, eight miles of beaches near the river mouth, and involved building some 45 miles of new sewers. The scheme will have cost around £150 million when fully completed in the 1990s, and will serve over a million people. On each bank of the river an enormous pipeline or 'interceptor sewer' has been constructed, and all the separate major sewage outlets, that once flowed into the Tyne, have been led into these interceptor sewers. The latter carry the sewage, mainly by gravity, to a specially built treatment works at Howden on the north bank of the Tyne. At Jarrow a tunnel under the Tyne carries sewage from the south bank interceptor to the Howden works. At Howden the sewage from both interceptors undergoes 'primary treatment', which removes about a third of the organic pollution by passing the sewage through sedimentation tanks and allowing 'sludge'

to settle out. The sludge is stored in tanks and pumped aboard a specially constructed vessel, the *Northumbrian Water*, which is 73 metres long and can carry up to 1500 tons of sludge. *Northumbrian Water* makes daily trips to a special dumping ground six to eight miles out in the North Sea, where the sludge is released through hydraulic valves in the bottom of the ship. The state of the sea-bed is monitored using underwater video equipment and the Northumbrian Water Authority claimed that 'marine life in the area has been virtually unaffected during six years of dumping'. The sludge storage tanks at Howden are large enough to cover delays of up to 18 days, in case the ship breaks down or is unable to go to

sea because of bad weather.

This ambitious scheme has been a success. Today the river no longer smells, new houses and apartments are being built along tidal reaches, and people sail and canoe without fear of septic pneumonia. The board's original objective has been fulfilled. Salmon are returning but not yet in the same numbers as a hundred years ago. In 1987 over 1000 salmon were taken by holders of salmon rod-licences, but there were also nearly 1500 licences issued. Thus the number of salmon caught per rod-licence was less than one, a figure that compares poorly with the ten per rod-licence that prevailed at one time in the 1880s. There is room for improvement: the tidal Tyne is still

ROD CATCHES

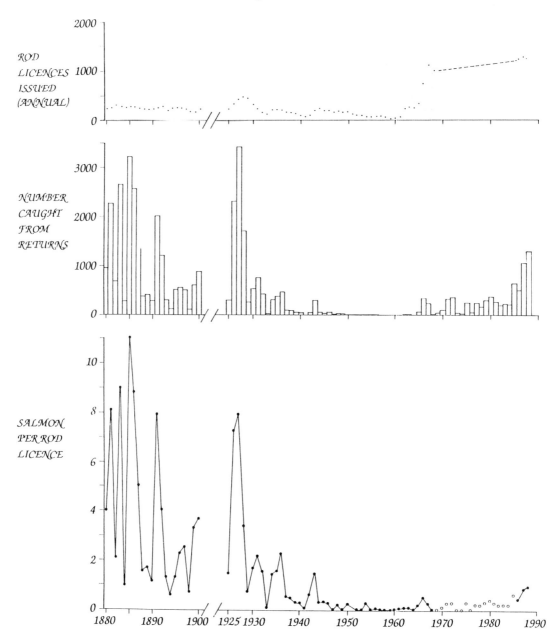

ROD
LICENCES
ISSUED
(ANNUAL)

NUMBER
CAUGHT
FROM
RETURNS

SALMON
PER ROD
LICENCE

The number of salmon caught per rod licence issued, one of the best figures to use when deciding how well a river is fishing. Note how the 1980s compare badly with the 1880s. (Mistakes and errors in the salmon returns are estimated at around 20 per cent. The dashed lines indicate the estimated total number of salmon licences issued during a period when data were not available.)

NET CATCHES

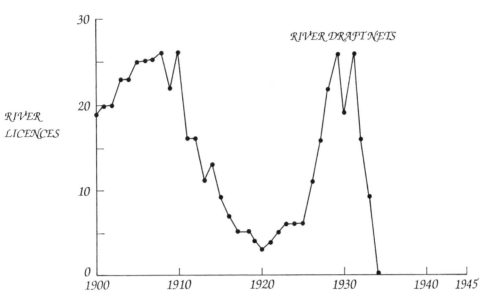

RIVER LICENCES

RIVER DRAFT NETS

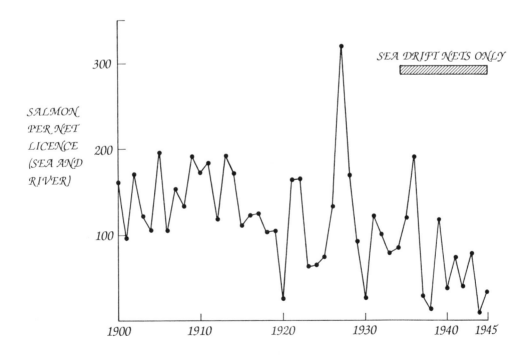

SALMON PER NET LICENCE (SEA AND RIVER)

SEA DRIFT NETS ONLY

Salmon caught per net licence issued, during the Tyne's decline. TOP: The final fall of the river netsmen BOTTOM: Salmon caught by each licencee. After the 1930s only the coble drift-netsmen fishing off the north-east coast caught salmon.

polluted; numerous reported pollutions are unprosecuted; and the average number of fish caught per angler is still low compared with major salmon rivers in Scotland. But the salmon are back in the Tyne, and migratory fish can enter the estuary at all states of the tide and pass through the once impassable barrier of the lower reaches.

It is not only Tyne anglers who benefit. Commercial fishermen gain as salmon runs increase. At Newbiggin, a town just north of the river entrance, there were 18 cobles drift-netting for salmon in 1927. The numbers dropped in the 1950s when catches were very poor, but rose again in 1970 when catches improved and some 37,000 salmon were caught. In 1989 there were 12 Newbiggin boats drift-netting for Tyne salmon. Today there is discord between angler and netsman, as there was in the nineteenth century, but many anglers recognise that drift-netting for salmon is an important source of income for Northumberland's coastal fishermen – without it some north-east fishing communities would not be viable. Drift-netting from open boats is a difficult and dangerous occupation, and the history of every fishing village is full of tales of drowned men and boys; even today, drownings occur with alarming frequency. In 1992 the long-term fate of the drift-netsman hangs in the balance; for the Government considers that it is 'desirable to phase out the drift-net fishery, but gradually so as not to cause unnecessary hardship'.

Fishing at night with heavy hemp drift nets ceased in the 1960s when nylon monofilament was introduced. Nylon drift nets are almost invisible in the water and can be worked by day. Their use is strictly controlled by the National Rivers Authority, Northumbria Region, which issues a fixed number of licences to professional inshore fishermen. The licences are much sought after and usually handed down from father to son.

During the salmon season, to conserve stocks, netsmen are banned from fishing over the weekend. The maximum allowable net length is 600 yards, and the depth has to be less than 40 meshes – each mesh being 10 inches wide. Nylon drift nets are comparatively easy to work, and once a salmon strikes the net the fish is quickly removed by the fishermen. Salmon caught this way taste as good as those taken by an angler in the river in the early spring.

Salmon, a luxury fish since the Middle Ages, continues to fetch high prices and poachers have been quick to see the advantage of using nylon nets. At sea the National Rivers Authority, Northumbria Region's fast patrol vessel is constantly searching for illegal netsmen and nets, while ashore the authority's bailiffs watch for drift nets run out from the beach. It is sometimes said that 'some of the region's best bailiffs are the licensed salmon fishermen', since it is in their interest to conserve returning fish.

Nylon drift nets are sometimes used by river poachers, attracted to a cleaned-up Tyne. It is no longer the case of a countryman taking 'one for the cooking pot': salmon poachers are organised in gangs that sell illegally caught fish at outlets hundreds of miles away from the Tyne, in London or the Midlands. Gangs may contain eight or nine men who work at night, sometimes using an inflatable dinghy to stretch a net right across the river; once the net is in position, the men wait, well hidden, for the fish to catch themselves. Other more daring gangs will drag a net right through a pool. Recently a drift net, probably stolen by the poachers from a coble, was swept through a salmon pool at the village of Wylam. It yielded more than 40 migratory fish, but the poachers were foiled as the net snagged, preventing them from retrieving it and its catch. Netting is not the only method used to poach

Tyne salmon. Other techniques include the more traditional salmon gaff and leister; snatching fish with weighted hooks; snares; a variety of different poisons; and shooting at salmon with rifles as they leap the weirs. On its lonelier stretches the river has even been dynamited in an attempt to stun the fish out of the water.

The National Rivers Authority, Northumbria Region, employs seven full-time bailiffs to help police the Tyne (and the Wear and Tees). They are equipped with infra-red binoculars and special radios, and in 1987, when the Tyne yielded the best total for rod-caught salmon in England, they scored notable successes. The authority

prosecuted 114 poachers, and its bailiffs staked out and caught five well-organised gangs.

Salmon returns have not only been increased by a well-oxygenated, clean estuary and alert bailiffs. Large numbers of juvenile salmon have been introduced into the river from a hatchery at Kielder on the North Tyne. The hatchery was created to compensate for the loss of the salmon breeding grounds when the North Tyne was dammed to make the Kielder Reservoir. The reservoir was completed in 1982 with the aim of supplying north-east industry with water. Heavy industry was expected to expand, but in the event it contracted and there is now a massive water

The Kielder dam.

surplus. In times of drought there are never any hosepipe bans in Northumberland, and today the reservoir not only serves as a recreational area but also, on occasion, generates enough hydro-electricity for a small town by passing water through turbines built into the dam.

The Tyne is now a controlled river. Most of the headwaters of the North Tyne flow into Kielder Reservoir with the result that there are fewer spates down the North Tyne and, to a lesser extent, the main river. If the river becomes too low in the summer months, the authority releases water from the reservoir to raise its level. The reservoir can also hold back water in times of heavy rain and help reduce flooding. But some salmon anglers believe that river ecology suffers from the lack of heavy spate-water; while others complain that sudden releases – for example when the dam is generating electricity – cause problems, especially to wading anglers.

Peter Gray with a stripped hen salmon at the Kielder Hatchery.

When the 44,000-million-gallon Kielder Reservoir was opened, its 170-foot-high, 3740-foot-long dam was clearly an impassable barrier to returning salmon. If they were to have access to their traditional spawning grounds, a fish ladder would be required. But the cost, estimated at nearly a million pounds, was prohibitive; moreover, although the salmon is a powerful fish, many doubted its ability to negotiate the face of the dam. And even if the fish had been able to overcome the high dam wall, a returning salmon might not have found any redds: much of the gravel in the small streams has been removed. Thus it was decided to build a hatchery not far from Kielder Castle, the old hunting lodge of the dukes of Northumberland.

The Kielder hatchery has a statutory requirement to produce 160,000 salmon parr each year – the estimated loss caused by the construction of the dam. The hatchery started

Stripping a hen salmon. 71

producing fish in 1978, four years before Kielder Reservoir was finished, and has, since then, been responsible for an average annual release of 320,000 salmon parr into the Tyne and its tributaries. By 1985 over half a million parr were being reared from fertilised eggs, and the hatchery was producing salmon parr for other north-east rivers: the Coquet, Wear and Tees. It was even rearing parr for the Tweed. (They were, of course, using Tweed broodstock and not Tyne fish!)

Each year, in early November, Tyne salmon are electronetted by the bailiffs. The salmon are kept outside the Kielder hatchery in specially constructed holding tanks where water from the Kielder Burn swirls through at over a million gallons a day. 'It's important that the salmon are not subject to stress,' said Peter Gray, the hatchery supervisor. 'We found that they are happiest when we cover the holding tanks with black plastic to give the fish shade. We also have to set water levels at around 4 feet. We know we have the right conditions, as the fish behave as if they were in the wild: they pair up, claim territory, and the males behave aggressively to other males who approach their female. In fact we have to keep checking to make sure they are not spawning in the tank!'

The fish are checked every seven to ten days to see if they are ready to spawn. It is cold, wet work and outside temperatures drop to near or below freezing. The hatchery lies deep in the valley of the Kielder Burn; in winter the northern sun is so low that it hardly enters the valley. Icy north-east winds blow straight along the Kielder Burn from bleak Kielderhead Moor, freezing northerlies rush down from high Deadwater Fell and Ravenshill Moor. In 1981 the outside temperature fell to −28°C to reach a high of −16°C at noon. Kielder Burn iced over, covered with a foot of snow, but underneath the snow the burn kept flowing,

supplying the hatchery with life-creating water. Outside, the men work standing with their shirt-sleeves rolled up, their arms and chests soaked in cold water and fish slime. They are continually buffeted by November winds with chill factors tens of degrees below freezing. Bailiffs have to pass through a 'pain barrier' if they wish to continue stripping the fish.

Holding a wet 30-lb. cock salmon that has come straight from the holding tank requires skill; the fish is slippery in its coat of protective mucus, and a powerful tail fin beats and delivers stinging slaps to bared arms if it is not quickly brought under control. The men tire and can suffer from exposure: open-fingered woollen mittens help them to grip the fish, but give little protection against the biting cold winds. For the first few fish, finger pain is agonising, but hands soon become numb as the pain barrier is crossed. 'We've had big, powerful bailiffs here – men fearless when dealing with poachers in the middle of a winter's night – just pass out with the cold on this job. I can strip any of these fish,' said Mr Gray, 'but if I do and it's too early, the eggs will not fertilise.' He picked up a fish just netted from the holding tank (sometimes local anglers help to net the salmon 'because we like to see these wonderful fish') and gently arched the salmon's back. If the vent protrudes, the fish is ripe for stripping. 'I can just feel when it's ready to produce; after 25 years you get to know these things.'

Male and female salmon with protruding vents (and thus ripe for stripping) are carried into the hatchery in plastic dustbins. It takes about fifteen 14-lb. fish for Mr Gray to obtain his quota for the River Tyne. A 14-lb. hen salmon will give about 11,000 eggs (around 800 eggs per pound of hen fish), and so efficient is the hatchery that over 90 per cent of these eggs will yield young fish. Any salmon that were captured by the bailiffs but not coming on to spawn in November or early December will be returned to the Tyne to breed in the wild.

'It's the squirt that counts,' said Peter Gray one cold November morning at the Kielder hatchery. He has been a bailiff, a fish farmer and a superintendent for the Northumbrian River and Water Authorities, and has worked for them for over 25 years. He was demonstrating the technique of '*in vitro* fertilisation' and skilfully, gently massaged the underbelly of a large cock salmon, working his hands from its head down to its tail. 'A 3-pound cock salmon is as good as a 30-pounder when it comes to fertilising these eggs, as a few drops of milt contain millions and millions of sperm.'

Each year in late November and early December, Peter Gray and Gordon Earsman strip sperm and eggs from the stock of electronetted Tyne salmon. Inside the hatchery they are surrounded by dozens of tanks through which Kielder Burn water gurgles at a flow rate of over five million gallons a day. The cold burn-water acts 'as a radiator in reverse', so that in winter it costs hundreds of pounds to keep room temperatures above freezing. 'It has to be warmer than 38°F in here for the eggs to develop once they have been fertilised. If the water in the troughs freezes and the eggs are touched by ice they are dead; it's the same in the hatchery as it is outside on the redds,' said Mr Gray.

Peter Gray, dressed in a green waterproof apron, looks like a surgeon under the hatchery's bright neon lights. His assistant swabs dry the fishes' vents, like a nurse disinfecting a patient's skin before the first scalpel cut. Within minutes his powerful hands reduce a female's round, tight belly, plump with eggs, to a flabby sac, the eggs shooting out of the salmon's vent in a bright orange stream, to lie glistening under the hatchery lights in a clinical-white plastic container. Eggs from two or three fish are stripped, to half-fill each container, and then mixed with the milt from two or three cock salmon in order to ensure that there is a 'good mix of genes'. As soon as burn-water is added to the mix, and not before, the sperm starts to fertilise the eggs. 'It's all over in seconds,' said Mr Gray. 'Sad, isn't it?'

The fertilised eggs are sticky, covered with a natural adhesive produced by the hen salmon: an important survival mechanism in the wild where the eggs need to adhere to the gravel in the redds to avoid being swept downstream by sudden spates. But in the hatchery sticky eggs are difficult to handle, so immediately after fertilisation they are gently washed. Any white, infertile eggs are removed before the eggs are counted, 1000 at a time, into stainless steel egg-trays, each tray holding 20,000 eggs. The day after fertilisation the eggs can still be moved, and any more white eggs excluded. After a week, however, only superficial white eggs can be removed. The developing eggs must not be disturbed until they reach the 'eyed-ova' stage. One accidental knock, and 20,000 eggs can be destroyed. 'Fertilised eggs are £35 per 1000 – if we have to buy in, it's an expensive knock,' said Mr Gray. White eggs are removed because they become infected with a fungus that, if left undisturbed, can run through a tray and destroy all 20,000 eggs; or even worse, fungal spores may spill over to infect the 60,000 eggs that are in the three other trays fed by the same water inlet. For five months after fertilisation, twice a day, every day, including Christmas Day, Boxing Day, and New Year's Day, Peter Gray and Gordon Earsman check the eggs for infection.

Within hours of being stripped the sea trout

and salmon are returned to the wild. The fish are carried down in oxygenated tanks from the hatchery by lorry to a release site downstream of Kielder Dam. Since 1988 some sea trout have been released into Bakethin Reservoir.

'A sea trout is more difficult to handle than a salmon,' said Peter Gray as he watched Mr Earsman toss a fish into Bakethin Reservoir. 'Its tail fin collapses when you grab a hold of it. A salmon has a much bonier tail and is much easier to handle. In fact it's a good way of telling the difference between a salmon and a sea trout: if the tail collapses when you grab it, you have a sea trout. It's surprising how many anglers mistake a sea trout for a salmon, and that's because there's not one clear identifying feature. But there are a number of pointers. For example, besides being bonier, a salmon's tail is more forked than a sea

trout's. Sea trout have between 13 and 16 scales counting down from their adipose fin to the line that runs along the middle of their flank – the lateral line. Salmon usually have less, between ten and 13, but that's not a clear difference as the numbers overlap. Sea trout usually have more black spots around the lateral line than the salmon and, as we say in Northumbrian, "Sea trout have a big gobs." A sea trout's maxillary bone, the big upper jaw-bone, runs back behind an imaginary line drawn vertically down from the rear of its eye. The jaw-bone of a salmon rarely goes this far back.'

Bakethin Reservoir is connected to Kielder Reservoir by a weir. When the water in Kielder Reservoir rises high (to within 4½ feet of its outflow level), the weir is submerged. The weir keeps Bakethin's water at a fairly constant level,

Gordon Earsman releases a stripped fish into the North Tyne.

unlike the water level in Kielder which fluctuates with weather and demand. There is no connecting river system from Bakethin Reservoir to the sea, and once released there a migratory sea trout will never return to life in salt water. But stocking Bakethin with the stripped sea trout is not a callous act, aimed at depriving them of their freedom. In still, fresh water, migratory sea trout will evolve into 'lake brown trout'. That is Mr Gray's hope, since he believes that 'A sea trout is just a brown trout who takes his holidays by the sea! They are all *Salmo trutta*.'

The released sea trout will probably change colour and shape to become an intermediary form between its previous blue-silver, migratory self and the river-bound, muddy-gold brown trout – the non-migratory variety of *Salmo trutta*. The new lake trout will probably retain its sea trout's black spots, rather than develop the orange or pink spots that are usual in the brown trout. It will breed in late autumn and early winter, searching out redds in the reservoir's tributaries. The young trout will hatch in the spring, live in the small streams, and perhaps eventually return to the deep waters of Bakethin Reservoir.

Gordon Earsman always releases the stripped salmon into the North Tyne, a few miles downstream from Kielder Dam. The flabby, empty bellies of the females have already begun to tighten. The males are unmarked by their experiences in the hatchery. Within 24 hours the females will have returned to a more or less normal shape. They are now kelts or 'unclean fish', and males and females should return to the sea, following the same instincts as those fish that have bred in the wild. Gordon tosses the stripped salmon into the river, the fish twisting and writhing as they arc through the air in this man-created leap to freedom. Their streamlined bodies hit the water with hardly a splash, and with quick

strokes of their powerful tails they disappear, speeding away from their close contact with man, having served important, if non-Darwinian, roles in the survival of their species.

Watching the fish swim free Peter Gray recalled how, for most of his working life, he has been involved in preserving the salmon. 'When we stock the river with the salmon parr, I feel they're mine and Gordon's fish. We caught the adults, fertilised their eggs and had an over 90 per cent survival rate, the best in Britain, I believe. The fish don't belong to the water authority, or the anglers, or the Greenland fishermen or the Northumberland netsmen, just the river. I feel as protective about these hatchery fish as I do about those that breed in the wild.'

In the Kielder hatchery every year around mid-January, some 60 days after fertilisation, but depending on the temperature of the burn-water (the warmer the temperature, the quicker the eggs develop), two little eyes and a backbone appear within the eggs (eyed ova) and they are ready for Mr Gray's 'shock treatment' – designed to destroy any 'weakly eggs'. The eggs are tipped into a plastic dustbin which is topped up with water. The sides of the bin are then struck with enough force to send shock waves through the eggs; any eggs not developing properly turn white within seconds and are removed. The eggs are counted back into their trays and now almost every egg will be expected to develop into a fish. Depending on water temperature, but usually round the end of March, the eggs hatch into baby fish or alevins, complete with yolk sacs which will nourish them for a period that varies, again depending on temperature, from three to six weeks.

Mr Gray once had an unfortunate reminder that fertilised egg development depends on water temperature. He used to send 'ready-shocked' salmon eggs to Canada. The eggs were carried in inch-high wooden frames, each frame supporting some 4000 salmon eggs on a layer of muslin. The muslin was first soaked in water before it received the eggs, which were held in place in a mixture of finely crushed ice and moist moss. The frames were loaded into tea chests and sent by train to the airport. But it was not unknown for the tea chests to be left in station waiting rooms near hot radiators, and on one occasion the eggs hatched before arrival in Canada and most were lost. Nowadays, with the introduction of specially moulded polystyrene containers, fertilised eggs, sealed in ice, can be safely exported anywhere in the world.

As soon as the egg sacs disappear the operation reaches a critical stage: the young salmon have to be 'brought on the feed'. The free-swimming fish or 'parr' are transferred to large fibre-glass troughs (30,000 parr to each trough) around which burn-water circulates before disappearing down a centrally placed outlet. Each trough has its own supply of water which, after running through the trough, returns directly to the burn and so reduces the chance of any fungal or bacterial cross-infection between troughs. 'They are like big basins with mesh-guarded plugholes, and we control the cold-water taps,' said Mr Gray. 'In the troughs we have to bring the fish on the feed. For six weeks Gordon and I give the little fellows proper "meals on wheels", every half-hour, from eight in the morning to five at night, and then again at seven and nine in the evening. We feed them regularly, as out of the 30,000 fish in a trough at feeding time there might only be 1000 looking for food. We have to be there when they are hungry; if they don't get the eating habit they will die, just like teenagers with anorexia nervosa!' The burn-water has to be above 7°C as salmon cease feeding at lower temperatures. This six-week period is the most demanding, worrying

and difficult time for the hatchery.

As the salmon parr grow, they are graded into three sizes; the smallest fish will be released first. About September, but depending on growth rate, Mr Gray will release some 300,000 parr (about half of his total 'crop'), into the North and South Tynes, the River Rede, and the main Tyne near Corbridge and Prudhoe. Later, in early spring, he will release the rest. If the winter has been wet and warm and the parr have grown to 3½ inches (8.75 cm), there is a good chance that they will turn directly into silvery smolts and migrate to the sea between March and June. Some go straight to the sea, others take some months to drop down-river. If they fail to reach 3½ inches by early summer the parr will most likely spend another year in the river before they smolt and migrate.

The Kielder hatchery can produce either half a million parr or 200,000 smolts each year, but the hatchery produces no smolts as they take up more space in the troughs. Mr Gray considers it better for salmon conservation to rear parr, and thinks it unlikely that the Kielder hatchery will saturate the Tyne with fish. 'A hundred years ago,' he argues, 'there were tens of thousands of salmon entering the river each year to breed and produce enormous numbers of parr.'

Wild parr normally spend two years in the Tyne before smolting and migrating. Once at sea their destination is likely to be west Greenland, but the probability of any individual returning to the Tyne is small. 'What chance have they got?' asked Peter Gray. 'Over 1000 tonnes of Atlantic salmon are caught each year off Greenland, that must be some 400,000 fish. On their way back, they have to avoid the Irish nets, the coble netsmen off the Northumberland and Durham coasts, the Tay stake nets and river poachers. It's a miracle any come back at all.' But they do, and in ever-increasing numbers.

Between September and March large numbers of the biggest parr in the hatchery are microtagged (60,000 in 1988) by a sophisticated machine that injects a 5-mm stainless steel tag into the cartilage of the parr's nose. The tag has a digital code which gives the river where the parr will be released, and the expected date of release. It is a tagging process with high survival rates: recently 15,000 parr were microtagged in a few days in September, and when they were released in March the hatchery had lost only seven tagged fish. Before microtagging, fish were labelled with small plastic tags placed externally and attached by a thin wire under the dorsal fin – a technique never as successful as microtagging. Plastic tagging was a difficult and skilled operation and so fewer fish were marked. Also, once marked the tags were exposed and were easily ripped from the fish.

The adipose fin of a microtagged salmon parr is clipped before release so as to mark the fish visibly. Netsmen and anglers are paid £3 for every salmon with a clipped adipose fin shown to the National Rivers Authority, Northumbria Region. A further £3 is paid if the salmon's head causes a special tag-detector to bleep. Tagged fish furnish much information on the natural history of the Tyne salmon, and in the summer months the drift-net-caught salmon are scanned for clipped fins.

Tagging has also shown that parr generally return to the river in which they were released. Somehow the river water sensitises the salmon to recognise where it smolted, perhaps even down to the tributary. Thus parr released into the North Tyne may return only to the North Tyne as adults to breed. Mr Gray releases parr at different sites on the Tyne to ensure that salmon return to all parts of the river system.

After a microtag is taken from a dead salmon's nose a few scales are scraped off the salmon's

back. In much the same way as the rings of a tree give the tree's age, fish scales reveal how many years the salmon has spent in the river, how many at sea, and if it has previously spawned. Tyne salmon spend usually two, sometimes three years in the river as parr; then usually two, but sometimes up to four years in the sea. A Tyne grilse, a fish that returns after spending only one year in the sea, weighs between 3 and 6 lb. After two years in the sea, a fish weighs on average around 15 lb. A third year in the sea would increase the average weight to over 20 lb.

Although there is only one species of Atlantic salmon (*Salmo salar*), it would appear that different rivers have developed different 'strains'. Thus a Tyne salmon that runs up the river in spring (a springer) weighs around 15 lb., while in nearby rivers, the Tweed and the Coquet, springers are smaller with average weights of around 10 lb. Some fishermen believe they can recognise the river of origin of a fish, but Mr Gray says, 'There is absolutely no way I could tell the difference between a Tyne salmon and any other salmon, and that's after 26 years of this job!'

As employees of the Northumbrian Water Authority, Peter Gray and Gordon Earsman have the hatchery and acted as water bailiffs: creating salmon by day, protecting them by night. Peter Gray first joined the authority in 1962, at the age of 22, at a hatchery on the River Coquet that was later sold. As a young man he worked with bailiffs who had been protecting salmon for decades, and 'wonderful characters they were, full of great stories'. One old bailiff told him the story of an unexpected arrest made many years before. One night in a lonely stretch of the river the bailiff and his mate were attracted to the water by the flare of a torch. Stealthily they approached the river and made out two poachers, silhouetted by the light held above a good salmon lie. As the yellow flames from the poachers' torch were pulled horizontal by the gusts of the autumn wind, the bailiffs caught the glint of steel – the shaft of a gaff. One poacher held the torch, the other gaffed any salmon attracted to the flaring light; from their silhouettes they looked big and powerful men. Not taking any risks the two bailiffs crawled as close as possible, and deciding to each take a man the bailiffs jumped into the river, and ran at the poachers; they yelled at the top of their voices and sent up clouds of spray as they splashed through the shallows. The poacher with the light was shoulder-charged and the force of the impact sent the torch flying. By its light as it spun free the bailiff saw pinafores, one full of salmon. The poachers were women. 'The bailiffs helped the ladies out of the water,' said Mr Gray, 'but they didn't apologise for treating them so roughly!'

Late on that cold November day standing on the river bank below the hatchery, Mr Gray watched the V made in the calm water of a glide by a fresh-run salmon. He saw the fish splash and struggle to negotiate rocks and shallows, intent on its way back to the redds. 'Salmon need all the protection they can get if they are to continue to breed in the wild,' he said. 'They are frustrated by the river and man.' He recalled how he was once hindered by a cat in his pursuit of poachers. For some time, he and another bailiff had been suspicious of two lads who seemed to have fresh salmon to sell every Sunday. Lying in wait by a well-known pool after closing time on a Saturday afternoon, they had their suspicions confirmed. The lads appeared and climbed a tree on the opposite bank. They lowered a wire snare on a pole through the tree's overhanging branches and down into the pool. After a few minutes, there was a splash and a fine salmon emerged, struggling violently, its head firmly held in the noose. The

lads killed the fish and carried it off brazenly towards the village. The bailiffs had to catch them with snare and fish if they were to have a good chance of prosecution. Carefully withdrawing from their hiding place, the bailiffs ran to their van and sped towards the narrow bridge over the Tyne in an attempt to intercept the poachers before they reached the town. As they neared the bridge they saw an approaching car suddenly swerve sideways; its brakes squealed and it stopped on the bridge, completely blocking their path. A woman ran towards them: 'I've killed it, I've killed it, I know I have!' In the distance the bailiffs could see the two lads, plus large salmon, as they chatted and gently strolled homewards in the warm afternoon sun, quite unaware of what was going on behind their backs.

The distraught woman had run over a stray cat, and the bailiffs spent the next half-hour calming her and disposing of the corpse. But next Saturday, at the same time, the two lads climbed the tree and caught another salmon. On this occasion Mr Gray crossed the bridge without mishap, took a short cut into town and grabbed the poachers as they passed. 'No cat stopped us catching fish and fishermen that time. They were local lads who knew us and we knew them and we never had any trouble taking them in. In fact that was nearly always the case with local poachers; if we knew them they would always give up without a fight – with one notable exception. We knew where they lived and, more than's likely, their families; the problem was to catch them red-handed. We would try to take them by surprise, jump out on them, and this was usually enough to scare the living daylights out of most of them. I've seen full-grown men freeze, like rabbits startled by the headlights of a car. Others would leap on to the bank and start running on the spot with fear, quite unable to move forward, their legs churning away underneath. But there was one man who haunts me still – he didn't act like the rest of them, sort of freeze when you touched them. He was completely relaxed when I put my arm on his shoulder, he just turned and tried to flick me off. Two of us each took an arm, both of us big strong men, and we managed to stretch him on the ground. But he started to roar like a bull, and his strength just grew and grew: he raised one arm and began to lift me bodily off the ground. It took about six of us to get him in the back of the car, and that was after he'd received a blow on the head that would have felled a normal man. When he was sentenced, he started fighting in the courtroom and had to be carried out, shouting all the while he was going to hunt us bailiffs down and then kill us!

'Nowadays things are changing. Poaching is big business and poachers come up here in gangs with nets and driving vans. We don't know their faces, so often they'll put up a fight to get away to their cars. I'm afraid we don't ask questions now, we're on them before they have a chance to be on us.'

According to Mr Gray, the problem is that there is always an outlet for Tyne salmon, regardless of the state of the fish. If a man in a Newcastle pub is offered a red fish, that has been in the river for months and 'tastes like wet blotting paper', he will pay a fiver for it – because it is a salmon. There is even a market for wasted and diseased kelts, exhausted after their breeding rituals, fish that are easily taken by the poacher as they attempt to return to the sea.

Peter Gray and Gordon Earsman have worked hard both as bailiffs and, nowadays, at rebuilding salmon stocks. Most of their days are spent in the Kielder hatchery where they are helping to recreate the Tyne as a salmon river. At one time Mr Gray was interested in developing a hybrid, and fertilised 10,000 sea-trout eggs with salmon milt. He produced seven 'salmo-sea trout' parr, but he never knew it they turned into smolts or even if they bred, as they disappeared once released into the river. Interestingly, there is good evidence that salmon and sea trout do interbreed in the wild (Mills).

Sea trout feed off North Sea coasts, and so avoid the wholesale netting that occurs off west Greenland. They are multiple spawners and, running inshore and being smaller than salmon, they have a better chance of escaping the offshore drift nets. These are some of the probable reasons why there are four or five sea trout to every salmon returning to the Tyne.

Nevertheless, Peter Gray and the Kielder hatchery are playing a very important role in the return of the salmon to the Tyne. In 1978, the year the hatchery started to produce fish, 200 salmon and grilse were taken from the Tyne by local anglers. Ten years later, in 1988 and after the hatchery had released some three million juvenile salmon into the Tyne, over 1300 salmon and grilse were caught by almost the same number of local anglers.

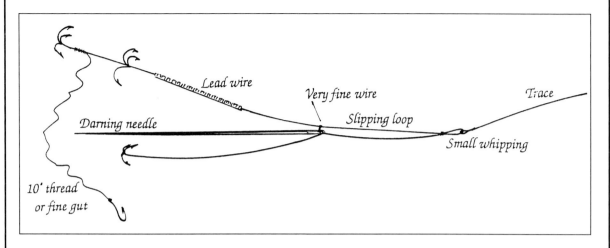

Lead wire

Very fine wire

Trace

Darning needle

Slipping loop

Small whipping

10' thread
or fine gut

Chaytor's prawn tackle.

A Day by the Side of the Fast-Flowing Tyne

Come, my lads, from your pillows spring, open
    your eyes,
And look out the best of your rods and your flies:
Cast care far behind you – let sorrow go pine –
For we swear we'll be off to the banks of the
    Tyne.

But, first, let the board be spread, ample and
    wide,
For there's no fun in fasting, whatever betide:
Let the eggs come in clusters, the coffee in
    streams,
And the ham, tongue, and fowl, fade away like
    your dreams.

Now a 'caulker', the finest, of rich mountain dew,
To add zest to our spirits and strength to our view;
Then away! like true sons of the angle we'll shine,
With our rods, creels, and lines, on the banks of
    the Tyne.

Where Newburn lies bright, in the rich morning
    time,
With its age-sprinkled turret, all calm and
    sublime,
We'll start like fishermen, up to the chase,
Determined no fugitive beats us the race.

Then on will we ramble to Wylam's deep holes,
Where the large heavy trout lie together in
    shoals,
And we'll hook them, and creel them, and make
    the glades ring,
As hearts, like our rods, all elastic, we'll sing.

Ha! here's Ovingham, famed, where the Great
    Bewick lies,
Once so dext'rous at handling the bonny brown
    flies,
As he roved, in his youth, by the sides of the
    streams
Which he afterwards hallow'd in glory's bright
    beams!

May his mem'ry be blessed where he lies by the
   side
Of his own rapid river, his glory and pride;
Few graced it as he did throughout the bright day,
And-so-fitting it is he should live in our lay.

We'll visit streamlets, decorous in mood
To think that we stand where the Giant One
   stood;
But, how sacred soever the streamlet may be,
We'll still hook 'the natives' with hearts full of
   glee.

Then Bywell's deep pools of some 'thumpers' we'll
   drain,
While every new cast gives mirth to the strain,
And the salmon lie splendid and bright to the
   eye,
And they take their last look of the stream and
   the sky.

William Gil Thompson's late garland.
Newcastle, 1 May 1840.
To the tune of 'Derry Down'

Chapter 4

ANGLERS ON THE MAIN TYNE

Traditionally the tidal Tyne ends near Ryton, but in fact the incoming tide travels further upstream to just below the pool at the bridge at Wylam. From Wylam Bridge the main freshwater Tyne passes through the villages of Ovingham, Prudhoe, Riding Mill, Corbridge and Hexham before splitting into the North and South Tynes. The main Tyne has not only been fished by wealthy and famous salmon anglers – perhaps the greatest was A. H. Chaytor who fished a beat a little downstream of Corbridge – but also by many ordinary fishers. By banding together and organising the non-profit-making Northumbrian Anglers' Federation they have been able to afford to lease and buy water on the main Tyne. The federation has given many Tynesiders a chance to experience the thrill of catching their first salmon, and many of the federation's young members have gone on to become skilled salmon fishermen.

Most of the villages on the main Tyne have angling clubs that have traditionally rented fishing at special rates from the local landowner. Some clubs have eventually been able to buy the fishing rights from these owners: one such is the Wylam Angling Club. From my window I can see the first non-tidal salmon pool on the Tyne: the Bridge pool. You have to be a long-serving member of the Wylam Angling Club before you can fish this excellent pool.

The fast stream out of the pool is hidden behind a large elm tree. It is April and the leaves of its upper branches have just emerged – tiny splashes of intense yellow-green that are sharply contrasted against a blue-grey Northumberland sky. The dark winter outlines of the heavier lower branches are already smudged by the strong colours of the opening leaves. There is a soft wind blowing downstream with just enough force to ripple the surface of the water. Occasionally I see the sparkle but cannot hear the splash of a leaping salmon.

It is balmy weather and there has been no rain for a few days. Through my open window comes the rich, peaty smell of the river. It is a while since the salmon season opened, on a cold, blustery first of February, and only a few fish have been caught. But now they are in the river in numbers – shiny spring fish, silver-blue and covered in sea-lice; aggressive sea hunters, their powerful 15-lb. bodies hard from long journeying and rich sea-feeding. Having entered the river they stopped feeding and after running upstream to spawn most of them will die – perhaps as few as five out of every 100 will return again. Most males will not survive; after fasting and fighting over the females they will have little strength to return to the sea. On the opening day of the season, in the lower reaches around Bywell, there were dead kelts everywhere. Many were lodged in the branches of the bankside trees, carried there by the winter floods; the smell of rotting fish was strong. For fishermen it was a good omen since these were autumn salmon which must have returned to spawn and restock the River Tyne.

I can see two fishermen spinning the Bridge pool. It is not long before a salmon is caught and brought to the net – the next few weeks should give these Wylam anglers their best catches. I shall have to wait until tonight, when the tide is low, to fish the first holding pool situated just

downstream of the village. But salmon never stay there long. When the tide returns the fish will run. Yesterday evening was mild and soft, as today's promises to be, and the tidal pool was full of salmon parr and smolts. They leapt high out of the fast-running water of the stickles, occasionally turning somersaults, as if they were jumping with joy at the prospect of their imminent voyage to sea. They grabbed hungrily, splashily, at a small hatch of March Brown flies. Perhaps it was the quieter brown trout, 'the-stay-at-homes', who only made the water 'snick' as they pulled down a spent fly or just rippled the surface as they sucked in a spinner.

When the tide leaves this part of the river it exposes a flat bed full of round white stones, like the abandoned cobblestones of a disused road. The tidal pool is reached after a difficult walk across these slippery stones and is seldom visited. I love its solitude. The only sounds are the rush of the river, the splash of the fish, the melodic whistles of mating blackbirds, and the occasional distant protests of a flock of birds trying to deter a local sparrowhawk. As I approached the pool a grey heron, heavy-bodied and slow-winged, flapped its deliberate path away from the poolside. Grey seals sometimes swim through this pool at high tide: a few weeks ago one was seen swimming downstream carrying a large salmon and leaving a bright trail of blood. There are increasing numbers of wild mink, and the rare otter, to be found along this stretch of the Tyne.

At peace with the world I had tackled up with a 15-foot carbon-fibre salmon rod: almost effortless to use when compared to the heavy cane and greenheart poles of the previous generation of salmon fishermen. Casting across the pool with a yellow and red tube fly and a fast-sinking line, I moved slowly downstream. After 20 minutes I had hooked and lost a fine salmon. For once

A fine springer, with sea lice, just caught at the Bridge pool.

losing the fish did not cause me to tremble with excitement and disappointment. It was a beautiful evening, fish continued to rise and I was still, more or less, at peace with the world. I fished through the pool twice, then through the lower pool, then the upper pool, but there was no sign of a salmon.

I rested on the stones and thought about salmon fishing. It has a wonderful grandeur – fishing for this powerful, magnificent fish with huge rods. It is not only hooking a fish that is thrilling; wading in rivers like the Tyne can be as dangerous and exciting as climbing a rock face. In floodwater it is easy to overbalance in the lower reaches, where unexpected holes and flat, slippery rocks await the unwary fisherman.

Why do I fish, especially when the probability of catching a Tyne salmon is fairly low? I thought of A. H. Chaytor, Tyne salmon fisherman and author, who 100 years ago must have been fishing the river only a few miles upstream from the tidal pool. He wrote that salmon fishing was not about patience, as most non-fishers believe, but rather 'It is hope, undying unquenchable, the heart and soul of salmon fishing.'

Any type of fishing involves being on a river bank, breathing the country air, usually away from people, towns and cities: being close to that elusive, indefinable 'Nature'. I often arrive at a river over-anxious to start fishing, and it takes time to establish a rhythm and lose nervous enthusiasm. Then, if I am lucky, the 'Ah, that's

A spring fish comes to the net at Wylam.

better' comes from somewhere, but too often it does not come at all.

Forgetting about salmon I had put up a 20-year-old split-cane trout rod, with 'Built by R. James of Alnwick' hand-written in indian ink on the butt. It is a beautiful rod, the cork handle grey and smooth with many years of use. Dick James chose his cane well, the wood grain runs true for the whole of its length: straight into the knots and straight out again. It is whipped with light-green thread which contrasts softly with the varnished wood, a rich deep yellow like the burnished gold of an old wedding ring. Each time I cast to a rise the rod flashed in the late evening sunlight.

But it was parr and smolts that eagerly took my flies. They had to be returned as gently as possible – the Tyne's future salmon stock. Salmon parr are fine-looking fish, with their forked tails, nine 'parr bands' and, along their lateral line, regularly spaced red and black spots. They were easily distinguished from a three-quarter-pound brown trout that eventually took the Greenwell's Glory at the end of my cast. The 'brownie' was thicker-bodied and wider-tailed than the young salmon. It had a red-coloured adipose fin, an upper jaw-bone that extended beyond the eyes, and its honey-yellow body was covered in brownish-black and red spots. Chaytor wrote that parr could easily be distinguished from young trout as they wriggled far more violently when lifted out of the water.

The bright-silver smolts were the easiest of all the young fish to identify. They left tiny silver scales in my hand, and their bodies were almost without spots, except for a few on the gill covers. In a few hours they would be in salt water and, as if anticipating their new life, they were snapping at the numerous tiny brine shrimps that darted through the gravel at the edge of the pool. The tidal pool is not far from an old salmon-netting station. But nowadays, despite the much

improved salmon runs, draft or any other form of netting for salmon is banned everywhere on the Tyne by a by-law that was passed by the Northumbrian River Authority in 1969. There is also a by-law, passed in 1975, that still defines a Tyne 'playground' area in the sea off the mouth of the Tyne, where the taking of salmon or sea trout by any form of net is banned.

Jackie Wilkinson, who was born in Wylam in 1915, remembers his father 'Ossie' Wilkinson netting large numbers of salmon from the Tyne at Wylam above the Bridge pool. There were two Wilkinsons and two Applebys amongst the seven Wylam netsmen: the head netsman was Sid Appleby. Jackie Wilkinson recalls that they would often fish at night, hanging powerful lights off the railings of the nearby station platform. 'Sid Appleby would keep a watch, and when he saw the shadow of a salmon swimming under the lights, he'd give a loud whistle. The men had just enough time to row out the draft net and catch the fish.' In the early 1930s there was always salmon in the Wilkinsons' house. Jackie Wilkinson, who spent the early part of his working life as a miner, said, 'When I first started, at North Wylam pit, I always seemed to have salmon sandwiches. I got so fed up with them that I'd swap them for anything, even jam ones!'

The Wylam netsmen later moved downstream, below Wylam Bridge, first to fish off Timby's Green, near George Stephenson's Cottage, and then close to the tidal pool. They stopped fishing in the mid-1930s when, like the Blaydon netsmen, they received complaints from Billingsgate fishmongers that 'Newcastle salmon don't sell – they taste of old engine oil!'

Alan Wallace, one of the longest-standing members of the Wylam Angling Club, was born at Crawcrook in 1923 and remembers the Wylam netsmen. 'For years,' he said, 'long after the

netting had finished, there was a little hut at
Close House, just opposite the Claravale pit, that
contained the old salmon nets.'

Alan Wallace's father was born in Shields and
like many young men would often row a small
boat out to sea. 'When off the entrance to the
Tyne, where the salmon got their first taste of
fresh water, they would leap right out of the sea.
Sometimes into our boat, but they didn't flap
about in the bottom for very long!'

There are many similar stories. One was
reported in the *Newcastle Courant* on 10 August
1782. 'On the 4th inst., as Capt. Boarg of the
Diligence of Whitby, was coming from Shields in
his boat, he saw a salmon leap out of the water,
which he wished would leap into his boat; no
sooner said than it did leap in, when a mate kill'd
it with a handspike, it is about 30lbs weight . . .'

Alan Wallace's father moved to Crawcrook and
Alan caught his first Tyne salmon. 'I well
remember it. We took it without a rod or line.
When the tide went out on the stretch of the
river below Wylam, the fish was left high and dry.
I was with my older brother and all we had on
were our short-pants and jerseys – it was a job
getting it home. But it was a great find, as those
were the bad old days, everyone was poverty-
stricken. As lads we would use anything for tackle
– branches, bent pins. We would search the tidal
water for hooks, turning up all the stones, and in
the end I taught myself to tie flies. Then the river
was full of coarse fish and trout, today they've all
but disappeared. The trout fishing was fantastic
and throughout the season I caught brown trout
on my favourite fly – the Partridge and Orange.
Nowadays you are lucky to see a trout rise.'

When Alan Wallace was a boy the fishing at
Wylam village was rented by the Northumbrian
Anglers' Federation from the local squire,
Christopher Blackett. But in 1940 the Wylam

*Mr A. Wallace and Bonnie, shortly after landing the
salmon.*

Angling Club was formed and the club took over the Wylam water, leasing it directly from the squire for a nominal rent. At first Mr Wallace helped the Wylam Club's ageing bailiff, Kit Pollard, to collect the annual subscription of 5s. and any entrance fees of 2s. 6d. Around 1950 Alan Wallace became bailiff. 'In those days the AGM of the club would take place with just four of us: the squire, the secretary, the chairman and me. The squire would get the drinks in, and the business would be over in minutes. Not like today when the meetings take hours!'

When Squire Blackett died he did not, as had been expected, leave his fishing rights to the Wylam Angling Club. After a legal battle involving British Rail, Wylam Angling Club finally bought the rights, raising the money by selling life memberships. Alan Wallace bailiffed a stretch of water that ran, on the north bank of the main Tyne, from Howdene Burn to the downstream end of Stephenson Terrace, and on the south bank from approximately 50 yards upstream of the old iron railway bridge to the junction of the Stanley Burn with the Tyne. For many years he kept fishing diaries, but all are lost except for one that covers the four years from 1978 to 1982.

The 1978 salmon season opened with severe frosts and heavy snowfalls. Alan Wallace's entry for Wednesday, 15 February reads:

After one of the coldest nights of the winter it got out a fine morning. I fished the Bridge pool and almost at once I hooked a large fish at the bottom of the pool on a large Toby. I was very lucky to land the fish as my reel froze solid while I was playing it, I had to hand line in the last few yards, and lift it out of the water as my tailer was also frozen. A nice fish of 21 lbs with a few lice. So a few fish must be coming through on the tides.

By 22 February the weather had improved.

I hooked a fish on a small silver spoon painted with red and blue stripes, the fish fought very strong and ran all over the pool without showing. It then showed with a number of leaps. I managed to get it on a short line and saw it was quite a small fish, it then made several more runs before I managed to land it. The fish had fought itself to death as it never moved when I lifted it out. The fish weighed approx. 10 lbs, and was a beautiful shaped fish, the back was a violet sheen, down to pearl on the flanks. In fact the fish looked like a large grilse for it had a decidedly forked tail. Mr Scott the Water Authority bailiff took some scales from the fish.

But by April the weather had again worsened.

16th April. The river is down to summer level, the weather is very cold with frost and snow. I thought I saw a fish in the B. pool and sure enough G. H. hooked a fish just on dusk in the pool. It put up a good fight but it gave him no problems, it took a small black and gold Devon. After about 20 minutes M. Jones tailed it first go, and it proved to be a huge fish of 31 lb. It was a cock fish . . . 48 in. long and only 22 in. around the girth . . . The large fish I caught in 1972 was only 43 in. long, but it had a girth of 28 in. and weighed 32 lb. after the guts and head had been removed. There are no signs of the sand martins as yet.

And on Thursday, 19 April 1978:

I saw the first martins and swallows, like last year they came together and have brought cold damp weather. It must be very hard for them for the hatches of fly are very sporadic.

The weather did improve. On Wednesday, 7 June 1978 he wrote:

I am very concerned at the lack of trout this

season, in fact it is the worst season I can remember. It seems to be the same story all over the river.

The diary continues into 1979, and on 8 April Mr Wallace carried out his duties as the Wylam Angling Club's bailiff:

Three youths were booked for fishing bait and taking sea trout smolt from our water. I took their tackle and phoned J. Watson who came down and charged them.

And a month later on 9 May:

The swifts arrived today, and the weather has turned a lot warmer. I'm afraid that the bulk of the fish have run straight through. The B. pool is full of dace and roach gathering to spawn. I caught a large roach on a Toby spoon while I was spinning for salmon.

A week later, on Wednesday, 16 May 1979:

The river is now very low but with rain falling as I write this we may get another flood. The river rose a few inches and I'm afraid what smolt there were tried to run and they all died around Scotswood. J. Scott went down and estimated that 3,000 died.

The diary continues for the 1979 season:

June and July were a dead loss as regards fishing was concerned, the river was low and dirty with the work going on at Kielder and Riding Mill . . . [but] the season ended with a good run of late salmon and sea trout. The river has been high all of the month and the fish ran straight through to the redds. Most of the salmon seen on the redds were large fish, some of them were 30 lbs. There were some large sea trout reported, what a pity that sea trout offer little sport, very few are caught on the main Tyne . . . November has been a wet month and there has been further good floods and there has

been some late runs of fish. There was a seal at Wylam for quite a while, I wonder if it came in with the run of fish.

The 1980 season opened well:

Friday 15th February. G. H. and I fished the Bridge pool for about an hour to no avail. I changed to a home-made blue and white Devon and I had a savage take on my first cast. The fish took right at the end of the pool, I hung on and managed to pump it up into deep water in front of the island. It fought very hard and deep and it was quite a while before we saw it. The first thing we noticed was the great girth of the fish in ratio to its length. After a few hair-raising moments and misses with the tailer I managed to beach the fish and we grabbed it and got it well back from the side where I gave it the priest. It was a lovely fresh-run fish with no sea lice . . . it was in fact 19 lb.

Three days later:

Monday 18th Feburary. G. H. hooked and lost two salmon early in the morning. One broke him and the other ran out of the pool. I think that is 6 fish he has lost, well that's fishing.

The Bridge pool continued to fish well during the opening month of the 1981 season:

Tuesday 23rd February. I got on the riverside to see G. H. lose a fish out of the end of the pool. I promptly hooked a large fish on my second cast, the fish made some very strong runs to try and get out of the pool. I hung on and broke my reel in the process. I got the fish above me and G. H. netted it out, it was a splendid hen fish of 24 lbs. Later in the same day Master J. Hagan caught his first fish, a nice salmon of 18½ lb . . . There seems to be quite a few large fish this week in the Bridge pool. G. H. has lost four large fish this week.

The 1982 season got away to a bad start:

We had a very cold spell during December and January with record low temperatures. When the thaw came there was ice left on the river bank to the height of 14 ft. The Bridge pool has altered quite a lot.

But improvement was on the way:

20th February . . . G. H. took a fish from the B.P. on Tuesday night and took two on Wednesday night. All these fish were taken almost at dark . . . We are having very high tides, I don't think I have ever seen the tide higher. I only hope it will bring a few more fish in. The seals are busy in the tidal stretch.

The Bridge pool also fished well in March:

Friday 19th March. I took a fish of 14 lb from the B.P. where there seems to be a fair few fish about. G. H. took another fish of 20 lb on Sunday. A. P. landed a nice fish of 21 lb from the B.P. and a fish of 16 lb was taken . . . on fly. The river is in grand order, very low and clear, the weather is cold at night but warm in the day. I am not able to fish a great deal as I am having trouble with my right hand. G. H. has had another good week with fish in the early morning and late at night.

On the last page of his fishing diary Alan Wallace wrote:

I saw the first sand martins on Monday 7th April. I lost my old dog Jess on Wednesday 7th. She got into the water and had a heart attack. I laid her to rest in G. B.'s garden under the pear tree. The river rose about a foot on the Friday and it brought a fresh run of fish. I am out of touch with who is catching what, but I was pleased to hear that 'young Kegan' took a nice 16 lb. with lice. The river is now very low with a few fish. About

Saturday 18th I got myself a new Springer Spaniel bitch. She is 7 months old, a beautiful beast, but I am afraid that she has had no training and has all the bad habits imaginable. I will try my best to train her . . .

A few lines later the diary finishes. He has not kept another one.

In 1989 Alan Wallace retired as the bailiff of Wylam Angling Club. But he continues to fish and every day, weather permitting, he walks his now seven-year-old spaniel Bonnie down to the river. The bitch is well trained. On Tuesday, 6 June 1989 he was down at the Bridge pool with his spinning rod and a Stoat's Tail tube fly he had tied himself. The water was low as it had not rained heavily for almost six weeks. Limping slightly because of his 'gammy leg' he cast into the pool. Within three minutes he was into a salmon. Only his dog watched, guarding his fishing bag, as he landed a beautiful fresh-run 14-lb. fish. The salmon's adipose fin was missing, so it had been released into the Tyne as a parr from the Kielder hatchery.

'With the water as low as this the salmon lie in the oxygenated water, but that's something you only know with experience. I'll give most of the fish away, to those who do me favours. As a pensioner it's one of the best ways I have of returning favours.'

'Big Alan' Wallace has been fishing the Bridge pool and the main Tyne for over 60 years, since he was six years old. (He once received a letter addressed to 'Big Alan, Wylam'.) He was a bailiff for the Wylam Angling Club for 35 years. The club's water stops at Howdene Bridge just upstream of the main village. Thereafter, through the villages of Ovingham and Ovington and, on both banks of the river at one time, up to the Bywell–Stocksfield Bridge the fishing was controlled by the Northumbrian Anglers' Federation. Nowadays, as Tyne salmon fishing continues to improve, the federation has lost some of the water below the bridge to local angling syndicates.

The origins of the Northumbrian Anglers' Federation go back almost 100 years to 27 February 1894 when a number of Tyneside angling clubs – the Isaak Walton, the Hexham, the Newburn and the Northern, along with the West End Anglers – met at the Chesterfield Arms Hotel and decided to form the Tyneside Anglers' Federation. The clubs elected a president and a secretary and ruled that the Tyneside Anglers' Federation was to be open to any angling club or angler. The annual subscription for each member was to be one shilling. The minutes of the first meeting declare the aims of the Tyneside Federation as: 'The preservation of fish, protection of fry and small fish, protection of spawning fish, prevention of poaching, illegal possession and sale of fish, and for doing such things from time to time as shall be conducive for the legitimate sport of angling.' The newly formed federation undertook a range of initiatives: it lobbied for a change in the fishery laws, attempted to restock the Tyne by building a fish hatchery at Barrasford, tried to abolish river netting and set out 'to obtain free water for the Tyne's coarse fishermen'.

Later a rule book was drawn up:
Any member of the Tyneside Anglers' Federation, committing a breach of the salmon Fishery Acts 1861–1876 . . . or who takes fish by any other means than by rod and line, shall be liable to expulsion from the Federation, and proceedings will be taken against any member taking fish by fouling, snaring, snatching, setting, trimmers, or using night lines or committing any breach of the regulations printed in the Federation Hand Book.

The rules were printed in the annually produced *Handbook and Guide*.

Thomas Bewick, famous wood engraver and keen Tyne salmon angler, believed that Britain's Izaak Walton clubs would play an important role in the protection and development of angling. Before his death in 1828, he wrote that the 'Honourable Society of Waltonians' should 'use every means in their power to protect the glittering inhabitants of the water from being unfairly taken or destroyed.' The Tyneside Anglers' Federation's aims and rules would have had Bewick's approval, especially its general policy of making more fishing available to more people.

In his autobiography he expresses strong views on this 'democratisation' of the river:

No reasonable plea can ever be set up, to show that the fish of rivers ought to be the private property of anyone. Can it be pretended that because a river, or a rivulet, passes through an estate, whether the owner of it will or not, that the fish which breed in it, or which live in it, ought to be his? . . . I have always felt extremely disgusted at what is called preserved waters (except fish ponds); that is, where fish in these waters are claimed exclusively as private property.

Nevertheless, Bewick was for controlling angling by fair means:

But as anything, however good in itself, may be abused, therefore some regulations should be laid down as a guide to the fair angler in his legitimate right, and some check imposed upon the poacher, who might be inclined to stop at nothing, however unfair . . . Pought nets ought to be prohibited, as well as catching of the salmon fry in mill-races, by putting thorn bushes into them, to stop their passing through, and then letting off the water. In this way,

NORTHUMBRIAN ANGLERS' FEDERATION

ANNUAL DINNER

AT THE

ASSEMBLY ROOMS
CROWS NEST HOTEL
NEWCASTLE

THURS. FEB. 15th 12.

CHAIRMAN, LIEUT. COL. ORDE. J.P.

VICE-CHAIRMEN.

JOHN HARBOTTLE. J. RUSSELL.
ARTHUR MUNDLE. JOHN S. THOMPSON.

a cartload of fry has often been known to be taken at once. Another method, still more destructive than this, is far too often put in practice; that is, what is called liming the burns. This ought to be utterly put a stop to by severe punishment.

In 1894 the Tyneside Anglers' Federation set up a Hatcheries Committee to improve the fishing, and in 1896 a hatchery was built at

Barrasford with money raised by voluntary subscriptions from federation anglers. The local railway company, the North British, was sympathetic to federation anglers and granted them special cheap fares. In its first year the Barrasford hatchery had '60,000 ova on the grilles, and the Hatchery is well worth a visit'. Federation anglers could obtain special day returns to Barrasford for the price of a single fare, namely 2s. 5d. But the hatchery did not succeed, partly because of a lack of good spring water, and despite obtaining £2000 capital when a limited company was formed in 1896. Barrasford hatchery closed in 1900 with the loss of all the raised capital.

In 1897 Coquet and Tyne anglers joined forces and the Tyneside Anglers' Federation became the Northumbrian Anglers' Federation. The minutes for the annual general meeting held in March 1899 state that 'the most important feature in last year's work was the taking over by the Federation of the Coquet fishing'. Prior to 1897 Coquet anglers were directly leasing fishing from the Duke of Northumberland.

In 1897 the newly formed federation had a membership of 700, and two years later this had risen to 798. By 1901 the federation was showing concern about the state of the Tyne. 'Statistics show a large decrease in the number of salmon entering the Tyne, and it may be that they are showing a preference for the purer waters of the Coquet, as compared with the ever-increasing pollution of the Tyne.' In 1902 the federation's membership stood at 505.

The Duke of Northumberland gave fishing rights to Tyne anglers on the North Tyne as well as on the main river. To control this fishing a separate Tyne Committee was created on 15 March 1906, with the Duke having the right to approve its members. (Its first chairman was the

From the 1912 Northumberland Anglers' Federation Dinner menu.

Northumberland miners' leader, W. Boyle.) The 1909 Tyne Committee 'appointed bailiffs to watch the portions of the river under their charge', and ruled that 'salmon and bull trout fishing in the waters demised to the Federation commences on the 2nd Feburary and ends on the 1st November. Yellow trout fishing commences on the 22nd March and closes on the 30th September.' Before anglers could fish the Tyne they had first to obtain a written permit from the committee. In 1911 the Northumbrian Anglers' Federation was again expressing its concern over pollution – the culprit this time being lead in the South Tyne, 'specifically from the Nenthead mine' – and was urging the 'Salmon Conservancy Board to take action from Alston downwards'.

On 12 November 1912 the Northumbrian

Anglers' Federation held a smoking concert in honour of a Mr John Harbottle who had been the federation's president since 1894. He was, rather predictably, given a 'fishing rod and reel in recognition of his services in the cause of angling in the North of England'.

John Harbottle was also a founder member of the Northumberland Angling Club. This club was formed in Newcastle in 1881 and many of its members must have belonged to the federation. Some fine pictures of these Victorian Tyne fishermen are still in existence. John Harbottle was the first secretary of the Northumberland Angling Club until he was replaced by J. S. Rea. The first president of the club was W. S. Vaughan, who was considered by John Harbottle to be 'the prince of fly-fishers' in the north, an

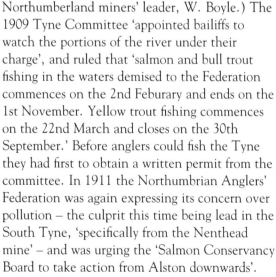

W. S. Vaughan, Tyne trout fisherman and first President of the Northumberland Angling Club (NAC).

J. Rea, Tyne salmon fly-fisherman and Secretary, NAC.

'artist of no mean order and well known in business as an able engineer'. A 'fisher's garland' written in local dialect, dating from 1883, mentions Mr Vaughan:

> On this speshul occashun aw'l sing ye a ditty,
> Aboot a grand club, in wor Newcassel city;
> Thay gan in for Art Piscatooral, thay caal,
> An a chep they caal Vaaghan's the head of them aal.

The garland continues:

> In the awd fashun'd days, wi nivvor had kreels!
> Patent Bumlers and Mennims, patent rods an' klick reels!
> Wi had nee flees i' them days, an as for a line,
> Wi elwis myed that wi' a bit grosser's twine!

. . .

> A've heard that thay've offor'd the Rivor Kommisshun
> Ti buy th' hyel Tyne, ti preserve it for fishin!
> An ti stop up the sewors aal th' way ti th' sea!
> Then start ti breed troots doon bi th' Bill Kee!

. . .

Secretary Rea was, according to Harbottle, one of the 'keenest North country anglers', a member of the Tyne Salmon Conservancy and possessed of a 'fund of humour as flowing as the streams he loves so well'. For years the Northumberland Angling Club rented water on the Tyne, but by the beginning of the twentieth century the rented waters were no longer available, and the club 'was conducted as a social institution, on similar lines to the Scottish and London fly fisher's clubs' (Harbottle).

By 1913 the Northumbrian Anglers' Federation was showing increasing concern over the pollution of the South Tyne by the River Nent and the inefficiency of the Warden salmon ladder.

In the following year, during the federation's annual dinner at the Collingwood Hotel, the president, Sir Edward Grey, spoke of the day of the poacher being past; but the chairman disagreed, believing poachers 'would emulate the poor in being constantly with us'.

Around 1936 the Duke of Northumberland withdrew the nominal rent he had been charging the federation for the main Tyne, and fixed the rent on the Prudhoe water at £50 a year. (Northumbrian anglers also lost fishing on the North Tyne in 1939 when the Duke's lease of that area to the Forestry Commission expired.) But the Federation was not solely dependent on the Duke of Northumberland for water. By 1938 it was leasing a section of the main Tyne at

W. Reynolds, President of the NAC in 1904, seen here spinning for Tyne salmon.

Stanners from a Commander Dunn, and in 1954 it bought the fishing rights (which it still owns) of the Ovington Salmon Fishery from Mrs Gibson of Bywell Castle.

The fishery commenced at High Stanners and extended along the north bank of the main Tyne at Alder Wood, past the old Eltringham ferry, to end at the Ovingham Burn. Thomas Bewick was born in 1753 at Cherryburn, within 100 yards of the river and almost opposite the Ovington Salmon Fishery, and he mentions the Eltringham ferry in *Memoir*.

The federation had become riparian owners, and along with the purchase of the Ovington Salmon Fishery came the lordship of Ovington Manor. Today lordships of the manor have become highly marketable commodities; feudal titles are bought and sold for thousands of pounds, many going to North Americans. There is even an exclusive Manorial Society for their Lordships which has some 800 members. In England there are about 13,000 manorial lordships, with the Duke of Northumberland owning around 200 of them. However, since the 1922 Property Act turned tenants into freeholders and did away with many of the feudal manorial rights, the titles give few benefits to their holders – perhaps the right to gather firewood, to dig turf or to fish.

The Ovington lordship purchased by the federation was at one time one of the manors belonging to the Barony of Baliol. An early reference to the title was made around 1116, when the tithes were recorded as being held by the prior of Tynemouth. In 1268 Sir John de Baliol had at Ovington '8 freeholders . . . and . . . they held 126 acres in parcels and paid yearly 15s. ½d. There were also 16 villeins, each whom held 24 acres, and paid yearly 10s.; and there were 16 acres parcelled among these villeins paying yearly 8s. . . . There were also 3 cottars

each holding a cottage and 3 acres of land, paying yearly for all 3s. 6d. The brewery paid 10s. yearly.'

The Barony of Baliol passed to Ralph de Nevill in the fourteenth century, and in 1398 his grandson was created Earl of Westmorland by Richard II. Attempting an insurrection the sixth Earl of Westmorland joined forces with Henry Percy, the powerful Earl of Northumberland, but they were defeated and Westmorland died in 1584, after living 'in the low countries . . . on a miserable pittance allowed him by the bounty of the King of Spain'. All his honours including the earldom were lost. In 1589 the Ovington lordship was given away by Elizabeth I and after passing through various families it was finally bought by Charles Gibson of Newcastle in 1922. It was sold to the Northumbrian Anglers' Federation with a mile or so of fishing rights. The Lordship of Ovington, without the fishing rights, was sold in 1987 to a North American to raise money to allow the federation to continue its annual policy of restocking the Tyne and Coquet with brown trout.

Today the Northumbrian Anglers' Federation has a membership of over 1000 anglers (not all of them fish the Tyne) and its business is conducted by a board of management consisting of a president and the trustees. Since 1894 the federation has done much to democratise Tyne fishing: their water is still open to anyone who buys a current federation licence which, in 1989, was £27.50. Although the federation has been criticised for caring 'more for the Coquet than the Tyne', it is still a non-profit-making organisation which continues to fight for a healthy and unpolluted river. It aims to maintain high fishing standards, its bailiffs fight poachers, and it continues to search for new fishing water. Present-day Tyneside anglers owe much to the federation's almost lone fight to clean up the river in the 1950s. And many Tyne salmon fishermen first went fishing on the 'Fed. water' (as it is affectionately known) as boys – not all of them legally.

Keith Walker, born in 1942, is nowadays a respectable member of a fishing syndicate that leases water on the main Tyne near Bywell which costs 'A lot of money to fish for just one day a week!' In the 1950s, when just in his teens, he was trout-fishing the Northumbrian Anglers' Federation water just above Ovingham Bridge. 'Then it was a beautiful, enormous pool, with a fast head, a deep glide and over 8 feet deep in places.' He had caught six large brown trout; but he was fishing without a federation licence. He had been intent on fishing, but on glancing up he saw, to his horror, a bailiff who must have been watching him for some time from the opposite river bank. It was with a thudding heart and a shaking hand that he continued to fish. The bailiff continued to watch, and then slowly wheeled his motor bike across the bridge.

'Got your permit, son?' asked the bailiff.

'Sorry, I left it at home,' lied the young Walker.

'What's your name and where do you live?'

'Billy Jackson, Winlaton.'

'Be off with you lad and next time bring your permit. I'll be checking on you.'

Within minutes Keith had packed up his gear and was cycling off at top speed to Billy Jackson's house. Too ashamed to tell Billy, who had a federation licence, he left the illegally caught brown trout on the doorstep. It was years before Billy Jackson's mother understood. 'She could never work out why Billy had left six beautiful trout outside on the step!'

A few years later, but this time with a licence, he was dry-fly-fishing the same pool for brown trout. It was late April, he was alone, the river bank was deserted and there was a large splash: incredibly, a salmon had taken the tiny trout fly. The fish fought deep, long and hard and on a number of occasions nearly broke the delicate trout cast. After some 20 minutes, and near the end of the fight, a man appeared walking slowly along the river bank. Without a word he walked down the bank to Keith, who did not recognise him. The stranger picked up Keith's net and helped land the fish – a beautiful 6-lb., fresh-run grilse: a schoolboy's dream. As he slipped the net under the fish the man turned, caught Keith's eye and said quietly, 'You know who I am, don't you?'

'That moment will be with me for ever,' said the now middle-aged Keith Walker. 'I suddenly realised I had a trout, but not a salmon licence. The bailiff carefully unhooked the landed grilse and gently returned it to the river. I almost cried, it was my first salmon.' The event was erased from Keith Walker's fishing diaries, and today he is unsure if the fish was taken with a Greenwell's Glory or a Badger's Quill – his favourite dry flies for the River Tyne.

The late Maynard Atkinson, well-known angling correspondent and fisherman, also caught his first salmon on water controlled by the Northumbrian Anglers' Federation on the main Tyne – the section that once belonged to the Ovington Salmon Fishery. His very first encounter with a salmon was also on the Tyne's 'Fed. water'. As a young teenager he helped land a 13-lb. fish from a pool near the now gravelled-up Merry Shields stream. (The federation no longer leases the Merry Shields water.) The power and the beauty of this fresh-run Tyne salmon set Maynard Atkinson on a salmon fishing career that extended over half a century and was to take him to most of Britain's salmon rivers. He saw the 13-lb. fish and 'just had to go salmon fishing' – but he had no tackle. His father, a keen salmon fisherman, told him that 'as in life, you have to make your own way in salmon fishing. Get your own tackle!'

Self-equipped and 14 years old, the young Maynard Atkinson set out to catch his first salmon. It was a fine June day, the sky a deep blue, the trees a deeper green when he saw the swirl of a large fish in the Oak pool. He cast a small wooden Devon and felt the pull of a salmon, an experience that during his fishing career he repeated over 6500 times. After a long struggle his first salmon was on the bank – a 14-lb., fresh-run fish. It was a big fish but his transport was, as for most lads of his age, a bicycle. Feeling it 'rather ostentatious to carry such a salmon hanging by the handlebars', he took off his coat, slid the fish into the bottom lining of his jacket and set off home on his Royal Enfield. He had become a salmon fisher.

The following week he took a 16½-lb. salmon out of the same pool, this time on a small silver spoon. By coincidence, and just after he had landed the fish, the man who had first introduced him to salmon fishing walked by – but too late to be of any assistance. This time he was prepared, and cycled home with the tail of the salmon sticking out of the top of a large rucksack. His third salmon, a 17-pounder, was also caught on main Tyne federation water, but this time on a Silver Grey fly. Silver Grey became a *nom-de-plume* that he often used when writing on angling.

Maynard Atkinson was a keen trout fly-fisherman. His biggest Tyne trout, which weighed 3 lb. 13 oz., came from the South Tyne and gave him one of his finest fishing thrills, but he still believed that, of all the different forms of angling, salmon fishing offered the ultimate challenge. 'A trout has to feed each day to survive, but not the salmon,' he said. 'You have to persuade a salmon

to take, perhaps by irritating it, but more likely by stimulating a feeding reflex. It is full of uncertainties, and there are few rules when it comes to salmon fishing. There is one rule though – normally, the shorter the period the salmon are in the river the better they'll take. I've caught fresh-run salmon in February, traditionally the time for sunk lines and big flies, on greased lines and small flies. On one memorable occasion on the Tweed I caught a spring salmon on a single hook wrapped around with the silver paper from a cigarette packet. A few days later, and by way of an experiment, I caught a salmon from the same pool using a greased line and an undressed, single black hook!'

Maynard believed that fishing skills and standards on the Tyne could be improved if anglers studied 'the background to salmon fishing. The fishermen should get to know the lies, not be frightened to experiment with different techniques, and read A. H. Chaytor's book on Tyne salmon fishing which, although out of date, is still sound.' He caught 80 per cent of his fish on the fly and believed that when one is fishing the main Tyne, because it is such a large river, it is best to use a salmon fly rod of at least 15 feet. He used a 16-foot rod on the main Tyne, and as the river is not particularly deep he used a slow-sinking line in early spring and late autumn. When fishing clear water he believed that a small black fly with a touch of silver does best. If the river was low and the water warm he would use a floating line with a small Waddington. But he was insistent that there are few rules when it comes to salmon fishing: 'never be frightened to experiment' was his advice. His best day on the Tyne was in 1988 when, spinning in high water, he took five fish of over 17 lb., and could have had more. His heaviest-ever Tyne salmon weighed 27 lb., and his best Tyne sea trout weighed 9½ lb.

Nowadays the Northumbrian Anglers' Federation's water on the main Tyne stops about a third of a mile downstream of the Bywell–Stocksfield Bridge. Above here, to the confluence of the North and South Tynes, salmon fishing is either controlled by village clubs or landowners and syndicates. The next village upstream of the Bywell–Stocksfield Bridge is Riding Mill and here, at the beginning of the century, lived Drewett Ormonde Drewett, benefactor to one of the Tyne's great salmon fishermen – Alfred Henry Chaytor.

Alfred Chaytor was born in New Zealand in 1869, the second son of John Chaytor who was the great-grandson of the first baronet, Sir William Chaytor, of Witton Castle, Durham. Alfred came to England at the age of 15 to attend Durham School. It was arranged that he should spend his holidays at Witton Castle with his uncle. But nephew and uncle clashed and uncle threatened to send the young Chaytor back to New Zealand. However, Alfred Chaytor's second cousins, the Drewetts, came to the rescue and offered to look after the boy during holiday time. This was the beginning of a great salmon-fishing career. Years later, in 1910, Alfred Chaytor published *Letters to a Salmon Fisher's Sons*, dedicated to his benefactor whom he describes as a 'just man and a great salmon fisher'.

Chaytor's book is one of the classics of salmon fishing. In *Salmon Fishing*, published in 1931, Eric Taverner reviewed some 300 years of salmon-fishing literature and declared that

Mr Chaytor's book . . . has placed him in the very select company of writers on salmon-fishing who are of the first rank. He expresses the best practice of his time; he clarifies in simple and effective language the thoughts of many of his contemporaries; of traditional ideas he discards

much without destroying what had been proved true and of value; and he adds to the sum of our knowledge of salmon-fishing much that was original and was the result of his own fishing experiments on the Tyne.

Letters to a Salmon Fisher's Sons was to influence many anglers of his own and subsequent generations. Alfred Chaytor was one of the first writers to advocate sparsely dressed flies and to suggest that salmon anglers should limit themselves to a smaller number of patterns. In the late nineteenth and early twentieth centuries salmon-fly dressing had become an art, and anglers found the bright colours, intricate patterns and ingenious names of the hundreds of patterns irresistible. Chaytor wrote dismissively of this:

These names are themselves a comedy. Some are truculent, as Butcher, Bull-dog, Thunder and Lightning, Black Dose – carrying in their names the idea of triumphant compulsion brought to bear on the unfortunate salmon. Others are romantic, as Fairy, Silver Grey, Green Highlander, Golden Eagle, Snowfly, Kate. Others recall the deeds of legendary heroes, such as Jock Scott, Popham, Wilkinson . . . if a fly is neat and workmanlike, well shaped, and with wing and hackle dressed sufficiently lightly to play freely in the water, it is of comparatively small importance after what pattern or of what colours the various parts are composed.

The Jock Scott was one of only two standard, fully dressed fly patterns that Chaytor used, the other being a green Heckam Peckam. Otherwise he fished with a few well-tried patterns of his own design with which 'I should be well content to tackle a day's fishing, ay, or a week's or a month's fishing on any river whatever'. Alfred Chaytor used the Jock Scott in 'big waters, or in waters stained with mud or with peat from moorland streams'. He also fished under these conditions with one of his own patterns – a 'sort of Silver Wilkinson' or a 'White and Silver', as he sometimes called it:

Body: Oval silver tinsel.
Hackle: White poultry or one dyed pale blue.
Wings: Mottled brown turkey tail; large jungle-cock's feather over each wing.

If he was not catching fish with the above bright patterns, 'to make a change – rather for the fisher than the fish', he tried his 'Claret' fly:

Body: Rough claret wool and seal's fur with a ribbing of broad silver.
Hackle: Claret.
Wing: Mallard, bronze feather, or brown turkey; the wings should be set horizontally.

Or he used a 'Port-wine' fly:

Body: Port-wine coloured silk wound round very smoothly.
Hackle: 'Pigeon's blood' colour.
Wings: Turkey tail, either brown mottled or cinnamon.

When the river was low and clear he used the above Port fly, or a 'sober little fly . . . known to me as a "Gipps"':

Body: Orange-brown and then black seal's fur, ribbed with narrow tinsel.
Hackle: Black.
Wings: Dun turkey-tail strips.

During the 1897 season all Chaytor's salmon were caught on only four flies: Jock Scott, Claret, White and Silver and Gipps.

Chaytor's generous relative rented fishing on the main Tyne near Dilston Castle and this was used, according to one of Alfred Chaytor's sons,

A Chaytor disciple, Andrew Sowerby, casting a long
line on the Tyne.

'principally for my father's amusement'. The Dilston beat was about two and a half miles long, on the south bank of the river from about a mile downstream of Hexham to the bridge at Corbridge. About half-way along the stretch a tributary, the Devil's Water, enters the Tyne.

Today the Drewett beat is leased by the Corbridge Riverside Sport Club. Chaytor mentions that the stretch had a fishing hut and, besides other pools, he names a Boat pool, a No. 4 pool, and pools near 'Thorns' and 'Stakes' where the Devil's Water enters the Tyne. Present-day salmon anglers can identify many of these pools, but bank erosion and changes in the river bed have drastically altered some of them, especially Stakes, which is now largely full of gravel and small boulders carried down to the Tyne by the Devil's Water. (Today few salmon run up Devil's Water as there is an almost impassable weir.) In Chaytor's day the banks of the Tyne in the vicinity of the Devil's Water were well wooded, but many of the trees have now been removed and the bank is more open.

The benevolent Drewett died in 1909 and the house at Riding Mill and the Dilston beat were given up. In the same year Alfred Chaytor moved to Sussex but he continued to visit the Tyne. In 1914 he wrote a letter headed 'Big Tyne Salmon' to *The Field* and took issue with the angling correspondent who claimed that the record fish taken by rod and line on the Tyne was 37 lb., and that a 35-lb. fish taken in 1913 near Hexham was the record for a spring salmon. 'This is not accurate,' wrote Chaytor.

> I happened to have been present when that spring fish was landed; indeed I gaffed it for the fortunate captor, but I have also seen landed on the same water two autumn fish both larger than the supposed record fish. One weighing 38½ lb. was landed by Robson the Beaufront keeper, and one of the best fishers I ever saw. The other weighed 40½ lb. But I don't suppose that any of these fish is the largest ever taken on that river. In the winter of 1906 or 1907 I was shown and measured myself a dead salmon kelt found below the village of Broomhaugh which was 57½ in. in length and over 14 in. deep. This fish when in condition must have weighed over 50 lb.

Chaytor's *Times* obituary described how in 1914 he 'took silk, and then came the War. He was by that time 45; but he obtained a commission in the 8th London Regiment . . . he served through most of the War attaining the rank of Captain.'

In the trenches Chaytor contracted bronchitis and asthma, and almost gave up fishing after the War, forced by ill health to take up the gentler hobby of cultivating fruit trees. Just before his death he published a second book, *Essays Sporting and Serious* (1930), covering a variety of subjects ranging from his beloved fishing to 'Post-War Manners and Fashions' and 'Simpler and Less Costly Justice'. In *Sporting and Serious* Chaytor describes a series of dry-fly experiments that he made. 'As long ago as 1896 I had some extra big dry flies, March browns, alders and coachmen, dressed in order to try them on salmon lying in shallow runs and other places suitable for a floating fly.' He did not have a great deal of success, having few rises and only 'catching one 19-lb. salmon and hooking one other that got away. And those were not taken on these flies but on a hackled Mayfly.' Although unsuccessful, Chaytor's 1896 trials must be one of the earliest recorded attempts to fish the dry fly for salmon.

In *Essays Sporting and Serious* he had confessed that he was 'no "fly-only" purist' but argued that 'to use minnow, prawn, golden sprats or bait of any kind is only truly sportsmanlike when the

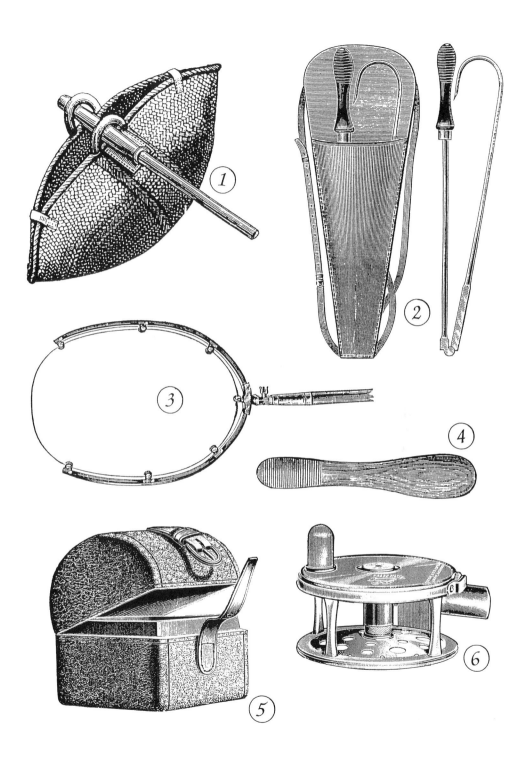

What the well-equipped salmon fisher would have used on the Tyne in Herbert Maxwell's time:
1) the 'Usk' salmon bag; 2) patent gaff; 3) tailer; 4) priest; 5 & 6) reel case and Hardy reel.

conditions are such that fly has no fair chance of success'. But by then his thoughts on salmon fishing were chiefly memories, 'for I am like Stephen Oliver, in 1841:

> My hooks are rusted; of my flies
> Consuming moths have made a prize.
> 'Tis three years since I wet a line
> In Eden, Coquet, Tees or Tyne.'

A letter in *The Times*, three days after Chaytor's obituary appeared, relates how the First World War had almost killed him. 'To those who knew and loved the strong, straight-talking, keen-witted, red-headed Alfred Chaytor, it was a tragedy to see what the war had done. He could hardly speak 20 sentences without a racking bout of coughing . . . and there was no sight more pitiable . . . than the greying emaciated figure.'

He died at Croft, Yorkshire, in July 1931, aged 61.

Another famous Tyne salmon fisher and author, Herbert Maxwell, agreed with Chaytor that the art of fly dressing had gone too far. In 1898, in *Salmon and Sea Trout*, he wrote: 'The popular theory encourages the extraordinary delusion that every river requires its peculiar combination of silk, wool, tinsel and feathers to take the salmon which frequent it. Thus we have Tweed flies, Tay flies, Spey flies, Usk flies, Shannon flies, none of which it is orthodox to use on any stream except that whence it derived its origin.' As an example Maxwell cited Francis Francis's *Book on Angling* where hundreds of different patterns were described and nearly all, apart from 17 general flies, were 'peculiarly suited, as was supposed, to most of the rivers in the United Kingdom . . . Thus Jock Scott and Wilkinson, which perhaps enjoy a wider reputation at the present day than any others, were classed by Mr Francis as Tweed flies.'

In *A Book on Angling* (first published in 1867) Francis Francis gave three unnamed patterns for the Tyne from a Mr Cook of Hexham 'which he states are not to be beaten, but are used with deadly effect'. The complexity of these is in sharp contrast to Chaytor's lightly dressed flies:

Pattern 1

Tag: Silver twist and gold floss.
Tail: A bit of tippet.
Butt: Black ostrich herl.
Body: Gold thread.
Rib: None.
Hackle: Two hackles are employed, a deep orange and yellow are run on together, all the way up the body.
Shoulder: Medium blue with teal over.
Wings: Two shortish toppings and a saddle feather from a golden pheasant with sprigs of blue, and claret swan, some tippet and grey drake, a little golden pheasant tail, a bit of peacock wing and another topping over all.
Cheeks: Short jungle-cock.
Head: Black.
Hook: 6.

Pattern 2

Tag: Gold tinsel.
Tail: A topping with sprigs of tippet, red, yellow and blue swan.
Butt: Black ostrich herl.
Body: Of wool, starting with yellow, merging into a warm medium red.
Rib: Fine gold tinsel.
Hackle: Golden olive.
Shoulder: Jay.
Wings: Mixed fibres of brown mallard, tippet, violet, red, yellow and green swan.

Head: Black.
Hook: 8.

Pattern 3

Tag: Gold tinsel.
Tail: A shred of tippet.
Butt: None.
Body: Magenta wool.
Rib: Narrow gold tinsel.
Hackle: Of a shade between magenta and claret.
Shoulder: Black.
Wings: Two coch-y-bonddu hackles, with brown mallard on either side.
Head: Black.
Hook: 9.

Herbert Maxwell claimed that he introduced the elaborately dressed Jock Scott to Tyne salmon fishermen.

It was in 1867 – nothing was permitted but sober greys, dun turkeys, and brown mallards. The gaudy, flaunting lures from neighbouring Tweedside were declared to be useless. This, methought, was very strange, seeing that Tweed and Tyne salmon enter the sea through estuaries not very far apart, and must occasionally partake of similar diet during their pelagic sojourn. Being at that time very fond of tying my own flies, and bright flies being more amusing to tie than dull ones, my boxes were stored chiefly with patterns like jubilee illuminations. Now it is far more satisfactory to kill fish on flies of one's own composition, so I audaciously disregarded the warnings of the worthy landlord of the Chipchase Arms at Wark [Tyneside, not Tweedside, Wark], who guided me to the pools, and met with brilliant success with Jock Scott and other flaring insects. At the present day bright flies are as fashionable on the Tyne as anywhere else, the Thunder and Lightning holding the palm, as they tell me. They also say

that the one fly which will not do on the Tyne is the Blue Doctor. It is no great pet of mine, but I only wish I might have as much fishing as I would like on that charming river on condition of using nothing but a Blue Doctor. I should await the result with considerable confidence.

The Jock Scott dressing given by Maxwell in his *Salmon and Sea Trout* would probably have been similar to that used by Chaytor:

Tag: Silver wire and golden floss.
Tail: A topping and Indian crow.
Body: Lower half, golden floss ribbed with silver twist. Above this are tied as in a joint some rich orange feathers from the throat of the toucan. Upper half, black floss ribbed with silver tinsel.
Hackle: Black cock's, over the black floss, gallina at shoulder.
Wings: Two heavy slices of bronze turkey with clear white tips, mixed fibres over of bustard, mallard, pintail, and scarlet, blue and yellow dyed swan, and green peacock herl. Jungle cock at cheeks, half the length of wing; blue chatterer over all.
Head: Black chenille.

Maxwell edited a later (1920) edition of Francis Francis's *Book on Angling*, and in it he makes a further reference to the use of the Blue Doctor fly on the Tyne. The late Lord Percy, a 'keen and accomplished salmon fisher', had told him that 'it did not much matter what fly one used on the North Tyne, provided it was not a Blue Doctor, at which the fish would never look'. Maxwell continues: 'I turned up my old fishing book, in which there was fixed a fly of that very pattern, and written under it – "Seven salmon in the North Tyne. Tied by the porter at Reedsmouth station."'

In this edition of the Francis Francis book Maxwell decided to leave out the earlier Tyne patterns.

Both Chaytor's and Maxwell's ideas on salmon flies were soon accepted. In 1929 Cyril Marson, in *Fishing for Salmon*, advised beginners to 'avoid purchasing ordinary flies as stocked by many unpractical dealers; they are invariably overdressed, and one fly will often contain enough feathers to dress three or four . . . I still retain, as object-lessons to avoid, dozens of flies bought over twenty years ago – useless, dense monstrosities.' Today most salmon fishers would accept the conclusions of two famous contemporaries: 'As to pattern of the fly this appears to matter little providing the dressing is sparse.' (John Ashley-Cooper.) 'Too much emphasis is placed upon pattern, and not enough on the amount of dressing a particular chosen pattern contains.' (Arthur Oglesby.)

Anglers were taking salmon from near Chaytor's Dilston beat on the main Tyne some time before he wrote his book – but not always intentionally. In 1870 an 'Angling Feat on the Tyne' was described by a local newspaper:

On Thursday evening last, while Mr George Robinson was angling for trout on the Tyne, at Wide Haugh, near Beaufront Castle, he hooked a salmon, with the near dropper fly, dressed upon the finest gut, which he eventually succeeded, without assistance, in capturing, after a struggle which lasted 1¼ hours. The fish was in the finest condition, measured 30½ inches long, 15 inches round and weighed 9¾ lbs, and was exhibited on the stall of Mr Milburn, fishmonger, Hexham. It had the small dropper front fly in its mouth when captured. On Saturday morning Mr R. went to the same spot of the river, and very soon hooked another salmon with the same tackle and similar

fly, dressed small sea trout size. He secured his prey in less than ½ hr., having on this occasion a small gaff with him. Its weight was a little less than 7 lb. The fish were male and female and evidently a pair. (Hexham Courant, 28 June.)

Around this time the keeper on the Beaufront Castle beat (on the opposite bank of the main Tyne to Chaytor's Dilston beat) was Mr A. Robson, according to Alfred Chaytor 'one of the best salmon fishers I ever saw'. It was on 12 October 1897 that Robson caught his 38½ lb. salmon on the Beaufront beat. The fish was 47½ inches long with a girth of 25 inches and was only just larger than the 38-lb. fish caught a few years later by Mr Hindmarch, the keeper on Abel Chapman's Houxty estate on the North Tyne. (The largest recorded rod-caught salmon on the Tyne was taken on the Chipchase beat of the North Tyne.)

Keeper Robson enjoyed talking about what he called an 'Episode in the Life of a Tyne Salmon'. In 1882, at an exhibition in Tynemouth, a fisheries inspector displayed nine salmon alive in tanks – eight males and one female. The female had a disease that seemed to disappear after six weeks in the tanks. The inspector, a Mr Harbottle, marked the hen fish with silver rings bearing reference numbers and letters and released the fish into the Tyne estuary at North Shields on 16 October 1882. The fish was caught some five months later, on 24 February 1883, by keeper Robson at Beaufront; he returned it to the river. Almost unbelievably he retook the very same fish about three months later on 14 April (Bolam).

Just upstream from the Beaufront beat on the main Tyne is the largest island in the Tyne, Broomhaugh Island, and nearby on the south bank of the river is the town of Hexham with its bridge, some 20 miles upstream from Newcastle. In 1908 Bradley wrote:

Hexham is a clean town set in a clean country. If you look over to it from the far side of the river, which beneath the bridge breaks into a broad expanse of rapids, in stormy weather turbulent and white with foam, with the old abbey standing out against the sky, and the long slope of the roofs and gables falling away from it on all three visible sides it seems a place worthy of ancient fame.

But the river was not so clean. In 1870 an editorial in the local paper defended the right of Hexham people to discharge their sewage into the Tyne, since the town had been doing so 'for hundreds of years'.

In 1870 local anglers were losing their fishing rights. A letter to the same local paper complained that the 'licensed men of Hexham had been shut out entirely' by the 'so called Hexham Angling Club' which had 'taken both sides of the river from Haydon Bridge down to Buck's Know'. The correspondent continued:

as to the happy time coming when the angling will be free to the public of Hexham, that's all moonshine; it will never come as long as anyone can get £40 a year for c. 2 miles of 2nd rate angling . . . The late Dr Beggs of Bellingham threw about 10 miles of first class water open to all licensed men, and this good gentleman was at the same time a 1st class angler himself . . . But we cannot run off to Bellingham when we have only an hour or 2 to spare . . . I have fished the above water for 23 years, but it had drawn to a fine close at last. The Hexham Angling Club have put a stop to it all at last by buying the right of the fishing, and it is a great shame that 7 or 8 men should put a stop to the pleasures of a whole town.

In 1870 the *Hexham Courant* also warned anglers to go fishing with both licence ('which salmon fishers will have to pay £1 for') and

'liberty'. 'Licence and liberty are two different things . . . I hear that any person found fishing who has not licence and liberty will be prosecuted, either by them [i.e. those who rent the water] or the landlord, so I think its best to let poor men and boys know the danger of going there to fish.'

In Hexham today salmon fishing is readily available. The Tynedale District Council sells permits on a daily or seasonal basis for a beat on the main Tyne at Tyne Green Riverside Park. The stretch runs upstream for about half a mile from Hexham Bridge to the site of the old Border Counties Railway girder bridge, whose wooden piers are still visible. This railway, a branch of the main Newcastle–Carlisle line, went from Hexham up into the North Tyne valley and carried many famous fishermen to the great salmon pools there.

A mile upstream from Tyne Green the main Tyne splits into North and South Tynes. A resident of Hexham fishes a private beat close to the confluence; his name is James Watson. For 24 years Mr Watson was the head bailiff of the River Tyne, and he still takes a keen and active interest in the river. He has fished nearly every stretch of the main Tyne from Wylam to Hexham, often as a guest. He has been a member of the Northumbrian Anglers' Federation for over 20 years.

James Watson was born in 1922 but the first river he fished, at the age of seven, was not the Tyne but the Coquet. He could afford neither fishing rod nor spinner; he made himself a rod, he learnt to tie flies and he became a fly-fisherman. Later he learnt to spin for salmon when a river was too high and dirty to fly-fish. He moved to Hexham in 1956 and, like Wylam bailiff Alan Wallace whom he knows well, James Watson believes that over the last 30 years the brown trout population of the Tyne has seriously declined.

'I think it is probably due to climatic changes, but other factors like pollution and the removal of the redds must have had an effect. One of the problems of a polluted river is that once the river is dead, no one seems to care. In the 1950s, when hardly any salmon were returning, the Tyne's spawning grounds above the lower reaches were literally dug out and the gravel, which had been building up since the Ice Age, was dredged out and sold for only sixpence a ton. Gravel was taken from all over the North, South and main Tynes.'

A letter sent by Major J. T. Gracie of Hexham to the *Newcastle Journal* supports James Watson's claim:

> *Before long the South Tyne will become a canal and . . . all the runs will disappear . . . The principal spawning beds for sea trout and salmon had been ruined by the taking of gravel. The natural food for trout, salmon, or parr, creeps, crawls, and hatches out on the bed of the river. This supply of food is being destroyed. The gravel removers will see that not an ounce of gravel is left . . . A considerable amount of pollution is caused for a long way downstream when gravel is being removed.*

'Fortunately,' said Mr Watson, 'in recent years gravel removing was first licensed and then stopped by the water authorities, but not before much damage had been done. Who knows how long it will take to recover? A salmon needs about a 3-yard stretch and about 1½ feet of gravel before it can spawn.'

James Watson has worked for three local river authorities since the Second World War: the Northumberland and Tyneside River Board, then the Northumbrian River Authority before it became the National Rivers Authority, Northumbria Region, and finally the Northumbrian

Water Authority. After the war, he was employed as an under-bailiff on the Coquet, and from 1953 to 1956 he worked in the fish hatchery at Rothbury before moving to Hexham to take over the job of head bailiff of the River Tyne. 'Then the salmon could hardly make it through the lower reaches of the Tyne. I had friends who lived at Howden who saw 30-lb. fish floating belly-up in the river, dead from pollution. Some years in May there were dead smolts everywhere in the lower reaches, great for the seagulls but the river must have been rotten. I heard it said that river netting stopped in the 1930s because the Billingsgate fishmongers complained that Tyne salmon were tainted with oil!'

In the 1950s, when there were so few salmon in the Tyne, James Watson and his two bailiffs were sent during November and December to the River Coquet to guard the spawning grounds against poachers. The Coquet bailiffs would have been up at first light to search for the redds, and by the time the Tyne bailiffs arrived the Coquet bailiffs would have had a good idea where the night's stake-out was to be. Mr Watson remembers with horror those nightly trips from Hexham to the Coquet. 'They gave us motor bikes for the 80-mile round trip. It was freezing cold work; we left in the dark, and came home in the dark after sitting out on a river bank until one or two o'clock in the morning. It was so cold that sometimes the milk we carried in our rucksacks froze solid in the bottles. Often it snowed, and one of us is lucky to be alive. He was caught out in a blizzard and skidded into a ditch, and how he ever got out I don't know – he was a little fellow and our bikes weighed about a quarter of a ton each.' In 1959 the bailiffs were given an old Austin van. 'What a luxury! Even though it was so old that I think everyone in the river authority must have learnt to drive on it!'

James Watson and the Tyne bailiffs worked long, irregular hours patrolling the river, their working lives dedicated to fighting poachers and pollution and to protecting wildlife. 'I was in one or two scraps, but most of the time it's the poachers who have the wind up – they know they're doing wrong. Most of the poaching in the upper reaches of the Tyne was by gaff and light when the fish were on the redds. I could never understand the poachers taking spawning fish, they are the future life of the river. Apart from that spawning fish taste horrible. I can understand why many of the villagers of the upper reaches prefer to eat tinned rather than fresh salmon!'

James Watson likes to catch salmon by fair means, and on many of his days off whilst working as a bailiff he was to be found fishing on some river bank. He must be one of the very few who continues to use a traditional split-cane rod for early spring and late autumn sunk-line Tyne salmon fishing. His 14-foot cane rod was built in 1960 by Ken Scott of Haltwhistle and cost him £10; today a similar rod would cost around £200. He also continues to use silk lines. He fishes the Tyne with a double-taper number 4 Kingfisher silk line, and employs the classic sunk-line technique of casting across the river at an angle of about 60 degrees to the bank on which he is standing. He allows the fly to sink and swing round in the current until it is directly below him. He waits a while, retrieves some of the line, and then moves downstream a yard or so before making his next cast. He fishes heavy spate water on the main Tyne with a large Garry or a Black and Gold tube fly on a 20-lb. breaking-strain cast attached to a treble hook. 'I use a 20-lb. cast as you never know when you might get a 20–30-lb. fish: Tyne salmon can run big,' he says.

For summer, low-water salmon fishing he comes right up to date abandoning cane and silk for an 11½-foot carbon-fibre rod and a modern floating line. He fishes for salmon using small low-water doubles, or ¾-inch or inch-long tube flies. He also uses the carbon rod for sea-trout fishing, and his favourite Tyne sea-trout fly patterns, usually fished with a 12-lb. cast and a number 8 hook, are the Stone Fly, the Wickham's Fancy, the Invicta, and the Cinnamon and Gold. If the river is very low he uses a number 10 hook.

James Watson is a skilled and successful salmon fly-fisher, like many others on the main Tyne. But when I think of salmon fishermen on the main Tyne my thoughts return to Alfred Chaytor in the days before pollution struck. With salmon again in the Tyne, his book continues to give much valuable information to present-day salmon fishers. It is indeed one of the salmon-fishing classics and Alfred Chaytor was one of the Tyne's greatest salmon fishermen. He aptly summed up salmon fishing for me: 'The very thought of a rod and a salmon pool can make one feel like a schoolboy going home for the holidays.'

Head of the South Tyne.

*But at that moment the figure of a salmon-fisher, with
a rod that could have landed a whale, broke upon our
solitude, and eyed us curiously – I fancied pityingly
. . . He evidently thought us to be natural fools for
throwing a trout-fly on the South Tyne . . .*

(A. G. Bradley,
The Romance of Northumberland, 1908)

Chapter 5

THE LEAD DALES

T he Carlisle–Newcastle railway line, built between 1835 and 1839, played a key role in the industrial and economic development of the villages and towns of the South Tyne valley. Soon after the line was completed the new goods trains transported lead from the mines of the 'lead dales' – the valleys of the East and West Allens and the South Tyne. These lead dales and the surrounding high fells and moorlands were once part of the North Pennine orefield.

The mines of this orefield have been continuously worked since Roman times. After the Norman Conquest the bishops of Durham owned many of them, and made money from both leasing and claiming royalties on the lead. The orefield was so rich that in the seventeenth and eighteenth centuries Britain was the world's largest producer of lead, and during the eighteenth and nineteenth centuries most of the population of the lead dales depended on lead mining. Lead production peaked in the mid-nineteenth century and mining for zinc, another lucrative metal found in the North Pennine orefield, peaked between 1880 and 1920. The last major metal mine in the Tyne basin closed in the early 1950s.

It was the new railways that fed and supplied the mining industry. With magnificent feats of engineering, the Victorians carried branch lines from the main Newcastle–Carlisle railway into the valleys of the Allen and upper South Tyne.

The Alston branch line was built in 1856, and crossed the South Tyne at Lambley on a majestic viaduct that towers over 100 feet above the river. And lead, by the thousands of tons, came down in the goods trains – from Allendale to Hexham, and from Alston to Haltwhistle. But with the railways, improved technology and industry came river pollution, just as it did on the main Tyne.

In 1913 Grimble wrote that the South Tyne 'is more rapid though not such a good salmon river as the northern stream, for its temperature is lower, and its pollutions are great'. And a few years later, the amateur naturalist and salmon fisher George Bolam wrote that salmon from the South Tyne 'were probably driven by pollutions from the lead-mines, in olden days, and their re-entry to that branch of the river is debarred by the ancient dam at Warden, up the old-fashioned by-pass on the side of which only Trout, in limited numbers, now find their way'.

The 'ancient dam' referred to by Bolam was most likely the Warden (Fourstones) Paper Mill dam situated in the South Tyne just above the confluence. The Fourstones Paper Mill was founded in 1763, but the weir across the South Tyne was not built until 1860, and the fish pass till 1867. (The mill race was led away from the dam and in the 1870s drove water turbines that powered the paper mill.)

With the Warden fish pass in place, and despite lead-mine pollution, salmon anglers in the South Tyne enjoyed the salmon bonanzas of the 1880s and 1890s. On 30 August 1890, at Haydon Bridge, it was reported that 'Mr M. Robinson . . . landed 2 salmon, Mr Hunter one. Mr R. Jordon on Wednesday morning had three salmon. The river with the heavy floods is in splendid condition for salmon fishing and reports show the run of salmon to be good and in splendid condition.' On 24 October 1891: 'Mr R. Watson of Haydon Bridge caught a fine salmon on Tuesday weighing 7 lbs.' And five years later, on 5 September 1896 '. . . Small grilse at Haltwhistle, and another at Bardon Mill. Numerous grilse and salmon up to 14 lb., have been caught at the water meetings . . . [the meeting of the North and South Tynes].' (*Hexham Courant.*)

In 1881 the Warden Paper Mill dam was breached by a powerful flood, then again in 1916 when the water level reached the high mark of the great flood of 1771 that destroyed so many of the Tyne's bridges. After 1916 the dam was never repaired; some 50 years later it suffered further serious flood damage and was eventually destroyed by the water authority. Despite Bolam's comments, it was unlikely that only sea trout could find their way through the fish pass. Once the dam was holed there were no serious physical obstacles preventing salmon from returning to the South Tyne – only river pollution.

Mining in the lead dales has left the South Tyne with a potentially serious problem. The early lead mines were shallow pits that were worked by hand, but the miners soon learnt to dam the heads of the valleys and release water to force off previously loosened earth, or carry boulders away from superficial veins of lead ore or 'galena'. It was a very powerful technique: tons of earth could be shifted and enormous boulders were carried hundreds of feet. The miners called it 'hushing', and by Elizabethan times all the major superficial veins had been discovered. The easiest of the surface veins were thus soon exhausted, forcing the lead miners to tunnel further and further underground. The Victorians developed increasingly sophisticated mining techniques and engines, and all were driven by a readily available source of energy, namely water. Miles of ditches were constructed to take water off the fells and into specially constructed reservoirs.

There was silver in the lead ore of the North Pennine field. The owners of the largest number of Allen Dale mines, the Blacketts (who later became Beaumonts by marriage and played a major role in lead mining for over 200 years), are said to have become rich from both lead and silver. The Beaumonts actively supported the Newcastle–Carlisle railway, since transport to the coal-fired smelting mills and on to the docks of Tyneside was the most expensive part of lead production. As a result of their intervention the railway line was routed via the Beaumonts' main warehouse at Blaydon instead of crossing the Tyne further upstream. The Beaumonts owned a huge smelt mill at Catton on the East Allen, and at the head of the valley, at Allenheads, the largest single lead mine in the Pennine orefield (Raistrick and Jennings). Allenheads mine was probably mined before the sixteenth century and finally closed in 1896. It had a series of reservoirs that could store over 60 million gallons of water which powered four underground water wheels that were used to pump the mine dry – so that paradoxically it was in *dry* weather that the mine was liable to flooding! Water wheels were used to drive the machinery at the Allenheads and Whitfield smelt mills.

Altogether there were over 30 lead mines and mills in the Allen Dales using water power to pump, crush, wash and sort the lead ore. There was water everywhere, all of it dirty, and most of it eventually ended up in the South Tyne. Although today the mines of the lead dales are worked out, this massive use of water has left a potentially dangerous legacy. Millions of gallons of water carried tons of poisonous substances into the Tyne which are still there today.

In or near the lead ore there were other minerals – fluorspar, quartz, calcite, barite, iron and zinc ores – that had to be cut away or washed off the galena. In or near the veins there were also copper, mercury, cadmium, gold and silver. The gold, lead and silver were kept; the unwanted minerals were left in spoil heaps outside the mines or washed into the river as finely divided ores. Some – lead, zinc, cadmium and mercury – stayed, and all of them are poisonous in high concentrations. Lead, zinc and cadmium have built up coatings on the fine sand grains of the river. In this form the metals are safe, but if the river becomes badly deoxygenated through pollution or summer algal growth, the coatings may start to dissolve (Macklin and Dowsett). First cadmium, then zinc and then lead would enter the water. As one university researcher recently said, 'It's like having an ecological time-bomb sitting there, in the Tyne!'

By the 1950s the South Tyne, like the rest of the Tyne, was suffering from pollution of a different kind. In 1953 the Northumberland and Tyneside River Board complained to Hexham Rural Council that they were polluting the river with effluent from sewage works at Haydon Bridge. A local paper reported that 'at present the stretches on the South Tyne below Haydon Bridge seem to be devoid of fish life . . . The Anglers' Co-operative Association, who have done much good work for anglers throughout the country in their fight against pollution, have been investigating pollution on the South Tyne.' (*Hexham Courant*, 14 August 1953.)

On 14 October 1955, under the headline 'Local fish are really patriotic', the *Hexham Courant* reported that because of effluent discharged at Haltwhistle, trout with red, white and blue backbones were swimming in the South Tyne. Haltwhistle Rural Council had insisted that an investigation should be carried out, despite assurances that such fish did not suffer and were just as tasty to eat as uncoloured fish. Councillor G. Dawson said that the discharge had lasted for between ten and 15 minutes and that the river had flowed a 'litmus blue and pink'. He added, 'This is where we get our real rainbow trout!'

Nowadays, however, the estuary is clean enough to allow fish to run up the main Tyne to the confluence, and most mining has ceased. By the late 1980s large salmon were being caught in the South Tyne, no doubt partly as a result of the water authority's restocking programme. Large numbers of salmon parr, reared in the Kielder hatchery, have been introduced into the South Tyne at various sites between Haydon Bridge and Alston, as well as into the East and West Allens and the Haltwhistle, Tipalt and Black Burns. In 1988 over 60,000 young salmon were released into the South Tyne and its tributaries.

In 1988 a local newspaper reported that 'with the rise in water levels on the Tyne system over the last week or so, rods have again been out in search of migratory fish. Fish have been taken right from Corbridge up to both the North and South Tyne rivers. Salmon in the tens of pounds have been grassed . . .' (*Hexham Courant*, 5 August.) And on 30 September of the same year the paper reported: 'Mr David March of Millersfield, Acomb, grassed a 31-lb. cock fish after a fight lasing 40 minutes. It took a copper spoon just down river from the meeting of the North and South Tynes.'

The North Tyne usually dominates the flow of the river at the confluence of the two branches at Warden. The North Tyne at 'the meeting of the waters' is much narrower than the South Tyne and tends to force South Tyne water over to the southern bank. It is probable that salmon, perhaps using taste, are able to discriminate between the two Tynes and return to the river of their birth. Salmon usually run up the North and

South Tynes in the spring. In the South Tyne salmon are caught from May onwards, while sea trout are caught from July/August onwards, and some large fish have been taken from this river.

An angler who fishes the South Tyne near the confluence is Ian McCredie. His biggest Tyne salmon was taken in the South Tyne in 1980, at about six o'clock on a cold, wet, foggy October morning. Tackling-up by the water's edge, he had seen a swirl. On his third cast the fish took – he guessed about a 9-pounder. After five minutes he re-estimated the fish to be 14 lb. and thereafter his estimate increased by 5 lb. every five minutes. After 25 minutes the fish came to the shingle and, as it rolled on its side, he saw the deep belly of a large autumn fish. It was a beautifully

proportioned, fresh-run silver salmon, 39½ inches long, 23 inches girth and weighing 26 lb. 2 oz. He hand-tailed the fish out of the river. It was so heavy that as he lifted the fish the vertebral column stretched: 'a soft clicking sound, like running a finger along the edge of a comb'.

Describing the joys of salmon fishing, Ian McCredie believes, 'There is nothing in the world like it, no thrill, no joy, nothing. When fly-fishing or spinning I know when a salmon is going to take before it happens. It's uncanny, call it experience, a second sense, I just don't know what it is. But by the time I get confirmation my whole being is euphoric, my thoughts become crystal clear, I suffer no anxiety, I don't become nervous, and I think I even slow my heartbeat. I

The meeting of the waters, North Tyne in the foreground.

have total control over the situation, and I try to eliminate all the possibilities of losing the fish. But once the fish is on the bank my knees go, blood pounds through my veins, my heart flies and I have this wonderful sense of well-being – my whole body is warm and glowing. If anyone asked me for anything I would say "Yes". I am on a different level, a fourth dimension, another planet.'

Ian McCredie was born in Newcastle and first went fishing in the Tyne at the age of nine. In 1965, 16 years old and on his way to art college, he took a summer job at John Robertson's tackle shop in Percy Street, Newcastle – and he is still there. John Robertson had opened the shop in 1959 and advertised it as 'The shop where fishermen meet and discuss their problems without being obliged to buy'. It was, and continues to be, just that.

John Robertson, who died in 1973, was a famous local angler and an angling correspondent of a local paper. In 1960, in an article in the Northumbrian Anglers' Federation *Handbook*, he discussed the pleasures of greased-line fishing. (Silk fly-lines were then made to float by greasing them with Mucilin, a patent lanolin-type dressing invented by an English chemist who was a keen angler.) Robertson contributed the article because he had often overheard fishermen say that fishing with a floating or greased line was 'much too difficult', but he believed it to be one of the easiest and 'certainly one of the most satisfying' ways of fishing. For the Tyne he recommended either a 12- or 12½-foot split-cane rod. He wrote:

Under the often bright and usually low water conditions one experiences during the late spring and summer months, when greased line fishing is usually at its best, longer casting is surely more of a necessity than it is when sunk fly fishing, say in the

early spring and autumn, often in slightly coloured water. One can only achieve this if the line is of correct weight to suit the rod.

John Robertson believed that after casting, one or two yards of slack line should be kept hanging off the reel and that when a salmon took, the angler was to do nothing except lower the rod point and allow all the slack to run out. Then the rod point was raised and the fish was hooked. It was good advice at that time as most fishermen would have been using single-hooked flies which were easily pulled out if the angler struck too early. Nowadays, with double and treble hooks, some fishermen argue that there is little need for slack line as compound hooks are very effective. Nevertheless, as always with different fishing techniques, there is controversy. Some continue to use the slack-line method, and others let line run out before striking. Arthur Oglesby, for example, fishes without any slack line, holding the line lightly between his fore- and second fingers, and when the salmon takes he allows a few coils of line to come off the reel before he tightens into the fish.

'Salmon flies caught fishermen' was a favourite John Robertson expression, and he believed that low-water flies for greased-line fishing were simply a matter of personal choice. In 1960 the most popular flies sold from his shop were the Hairy Mary, the Stoat's Tail, the Blue Charm and the Silver Blue. Tube flies were then just being introduced and the 'question of whether one uses an orthodox low water fly or a tube fly is also a matter of personal fancy – both are probably equally effective'. John Robertson's was one of the first tackle shops in Newcastle to sell tube flies and he soon carried the widest range and largest selection in Britain. When Ian McCredie arrived, the shop sold 100 tubes for every conventional fly.

In the 1960s a few salmon were being caught in the Tyne. The Kielder Reservoir was not built to hold back the headwaters of the North Tyne, and very heavy rainfalls were able to wash out the pollution in the lower reaches sufficiently to allow a reasonable smolt migration to take place; a few years later, salmon would return to spawn. There were some exceptionally heavy spates in the river between 1965 and 1970 and skilful Tyne fishermen caught fish. Ian McCredie caught at least two fish a year: 'Then you had to work hard for your salmon, as you do now. Although today the Tyne is much improved it's still not like, say, the Tweed. When I go to Scotland in the back end of the season I expect to get a fish – if I return home empty-handed I'm a very disappointed man.'

In the mid-1960s Ian McCredie, like most fly-fishers on the Tyne, used a 14-foot split-cane salmon rod with a double-built butt for both greased- and sunk-line fishing. He carried a spare rod top as they were easily broken, especially when pulling sunk lines out of deep water. The 14-foot rod was fished with 40 yards of number 6 Kingfisher silk line, which was attached to a flax backing (and is equivalent to a current AFIM number 10). For Tyne salmon the cast was of nylon monofilament, typically with a breaking strain of 20 lb.

He would have liked to be able to afford a 12½-foot rod for greased-line fishing, especially one made by the world-famous tackle manufacturer Hardy's of Alnwick, or perhaps one built by Walker-Bampton. In the 1960s many anglers could not afford a Hardy rod, and bought one made by Sealey's (who made rods for J. B. Walker). A typical reasonably priced, 4-inch-wide drum salmon reel of the 1960s would have been a Pridex made by J. W. Young. The top of the range was the Perfect, made by Hardy's,

which went out of production in 1965.

In the 1960s the depth at which conventional salmon flies were fished was altered by adding lead to the head or body of the fly. Tube flies were either tied on plastic tubing or on different weights of extruded brass tubing. For deep, coloured, heavy spate water tube flies were even dressed on drilled solid brass rod. Tube flies were dressed with hairwings, and dressers made interpretations of traditional fly dressings. There was a saying that an autumn tube fly's hair should be dyed to match the colour of the autumn leaves: red, yellow, brown and gold. The all-round favourite tube fly for use on the Tyne was the Garry or Yellow Dog, and it is still the river's most popular salmon fly:

Tail: Golden pheasant crest and tippet
Body: Black floss
Rib: Silver tinsel, oval
Hackle: Black cock hackle with blue-dyed guinea fowl
Wing: Red bucktail under yellow bucktail.

Ian McCredie remembers the advent of tubular glass-fibre rods in the mid-1960s. Glass-fibre rods represented a technological revolution, and quickly replaced split cane; between 1964 and 1976 fibreglass reigned supreme. To many anglers glass-fibre rods were far less beautiful than cane ones, and for casting they lacked cane's 'crispness' and directional stability. But they were much lighter, easier and therefore cheaper to make, and above all almost indestructible.

Carbon-fibre rods were another technological breakthrough. They were introduced in the early 1970s and today Robertson's, like most Tyneside tackle shops, sells almost only carbon rods. (A few split canes are still sold.) Compared with glass-fibre rods they are lighter, stronger, more sensitive, and less than 60 per cent of the diameter of a glass rod of similar length. They have one major fault: they have a low 'impact resistance', i.e. they splinter easily if, for example, they are struck by a badly cast heavy tube fly. To improve impact resistance most manufacturers nowadays either produce carbon rods with a glass-fibre core or reinforce the outer layers of matting with Kevlar, a substance that has 'phenomenal impact resistance'. Another problem is that carbon-fibre rods conduct electricity, and every year there are accidents with overhead power lines.

In the mid-1960s American plastic lines were introduced on Tyneside and they have captured the market. Some die-hards were reluctant to give up their silk lines. 'Silk lines were gorgeous, there was nothing to match the turnover or the presentation of those lines,' says Ian McCredie. 'But they had to be dried each time they were used, greased to make them float, and after a while, no matter how careful you were, they went sticky. A few people still use them, but soon they'll be museum pieces. No, it's a plastic line for today's Tyne angler.'

Plastic lines come in many different forms. An angler new to Tyne salmon fishing would, on entering Robertson's, be advised by Mr McCredie to buy first a slow-sinking line: this would be used 80 per cent of the fishing time. Next he recommends a floating line for clear and low water, then, in order of priority, a sinking-tip, a neutral-density and a fast-sinking line. He believes a 15-foot carbon rod would be adequate for all Tyne fly fishing, used perhaps with a number 10 line, depending on the rod. For summer fishing in low water with a floating line, he suggests using a double hook, its size varying between 6 and 12 depending on water conditions. He believes well-tried, traditional fly patterns with modern dressings are as good as any –

General Practitioner, Hairy Mary, Stoat's Tail and Shrimp Fly.

A question he is often asked is 'What fly shall I use, and when?' He replies, 'It's always a problem to make rules. But when salmon fishing on a dull day I believe any coloured fly will do. But on a bright day, a darkly dressed fly is best as it can stand closer inspection by the fish. I reject the more orthodox view that a bright fly should be used on a bright day. A dark or black fly is best for when the water is high and dirty, since it's more visible than a coloured fly.'

However, he believes that the old saying 'The colder, the higher, the more coloured the water, the larger and heavier the fly' holds for the Tyne as it does for most salmon rivers. He is happy to see the recent reappearance of Waddington lures. 'They are a refinement of the tube fly and much easier to cast, as those heavy brass tube flies abrade the nylon as they slide up and down during casting.' He thinks that Waddingtons are bringing back the skill to heavy-water fly fishing, as they rely less on brute force and more on skill when casting the deep fly. 'A selection of Waddingtons, ranging from an inch to 2½ inches in length, and dressed with black hair, or as Garrys, would be adequate for most conditions found in spring and autumn on the Tyne,' he says.

Ian McCredie is not a conservative fisherman. He has tried every conventional technique, and also developed a number of new ones. He both fly-fishes and spins for salmon, and over the years has had a lot of success with a spinning technique 'that is rather like fly fishing'. The technique requires an 11-foot rod and a multiplier reel, and he fishes the spinner like a fly, holding it over the lies and working it back to his bank. But like most good salmon fishermen, he thinks there are no rules. 'For example, I caught a salmon on a two-inch tube fly and slow-sinking line. Within a

few hours I took from the same lie a fish on a
floating line with a fly tied on a number six
double. To me, if not the salmon, the river and
the fishing conditions were the same. So it's not
helpful to think in a blinkered manner about
salmon fishing, you must be prepared to try
different techniques, even if at first they appear to
be inappropriate.'

A man who has tried a method that many more
conservative salmon anglers consider
inappropriate is Guy Hall. He lives at Allerwash
Hall and fishes the water below his house.

The technique is called 'dibbling'. Last century
Herbert Maxwell wrote of a similar technique that
was used by a Dr Begg on the North Tyne. Guy
Hall first 'dibbled' in 1983 and now it is his
preferred way of Tyne salmon fishing, being
especially effective when the sun is high and the
river is low. He was born in 1938 and first fly-
fished the Tyne when he was six. Both his father
and grandfather were Tyne fishermen and his
great-aunt was the first lady member of the
Corbridge Riverside Sport Club. For much of his
early boyhood he went trout fishing with his father
in the Tyne but it was not until the early 1950s
that he saw his first Tyne salmon kelt and decided
to go for salmon. He studied the works of Richard
Waddington and went fishing at Tyne Green,
Hexham. His equipment was a 16-foot greenheart
rod, a huge brass reel and an enormous size 8/0
single-hooked fly. His catch returns were nil.

Nowadays Guy Hall is a very successful Tyne
salmon fisherman who restricts himself to various
forms of fly fishing and generally catches the first
fish of the season in his local angling club where
he is a committee member. In early spring and
late autumn he uses conventional sunk-line
fishing techniques, but once the water
temperature climbs above 54°F, usually from May
to mid-October, he dibbles for salmon. He always

brings three carbon-fibre rods of varying lengths:
10-feet, 15 feet 4 inches and 20 feet. When
dibbling he prefers to use the 20-foot rod with a
number 7 Air Cel floating line and a 15-foot cast.
The first 11 feet of the cast, down to a 4-inch
dropper, are of Maxima nylon with a 10–12-lb.
breaking strain. He uses lighter nylon for the last
4 feet of the cast. On the dropper he generally
fishes with a very bushy Stinchar Stoat's Tail
dressed on a number 8 or 6 Esmond Drury treble
hook:

Hook: Esmond Drury, size 2 to 12
Body: None or lead wire
Hackle: Hot orange cock hackle
Wing: Black hair (bucktail, goat, stoat, etc.)
which is up to three times the length of the
hook.

For the tail fly he uses a fine-wired, long-shanked
size 14 treble, which is thinly dressed with a pure
black hackle.

In dibbling it is always the dropper that catches
the salmon. Guy Hall lost several salmon when
the tail fly snagged when a salmon was on the
dropper, and so he experimented by replacing it
with bunches of nylon or hookless flies. He has
recently returned to using the tiny black tail fly,
as it occasionally takes sea trout that snatched at
and missed the dropper but are quick enough to
turn and grab the tail fly. The light line and the
exceptionally long rod enable him to manipulate
the dropper so that it drags across the surface at
speed, making a clear wake. The tail fly sinks but
the dropper skates on the surface. 'If I can't see
the dropper's wake it's not fishing properly.' If
fishing with a strong wind he allows the wind to
blow the line out, otherwise he generally roll-
casts – a simple matter with such a long rod.

Under ideal dibbling conditions – low water,

bright sunlight, temperatures above 54°F, a light breeze and, most important, undisturbed fish – 'I can almost guarantee to rise a salmon,' he says. 'Tyne salmon are aggressive takers and will readily rise to the skated fly, but they often take short. It is almost a rule that I have more than one, sometimes even six rises, from a single fish before I hook it.' After the first swirl he waits for a minute, casts again, and then brings the dropper back even faster. With this technique, salmon become so stimulated that they frequently jump out of the water to snatch the fly – 'It's tremendously exciting!'

Guy Hall believes it is very important to approach the river carefully, to wade quietly and to wear camouflaged clothing. He works his way stealthily but rapidly down a pool, paying particular attention to lies and the shallow water at the end of the pool. He feels (along with his mentor G. P. R. Balfour-Kinnear) that salmon show interest at the first sight of the fly and thus his aim is to make as many 'first casts' as possible.

Each year he stops 'serious fishing' when he has caught some half a dozen salmon. 'I only fish for the table, and I don't want to slaughter salmon. In fact I feel rather guilty about knocking the ones I keep on the head. I can understand those people who fish with barbless hooks and return their catch; but I also sympathise with the enthusiasm of youth! Once I've caught my own set quota I try experimenting with different techniques – I have a lifetime of experiments out there in front of me.' He prefers to catch salmon. 'If I hook a large sea trout I'm ashamed to say I feel disappointed. There's something about a salmon: it hypnotises me, that low-set eye stares back, stares through me.'

He loves to spend quiet moments on the river bank, and often walks down to the river's edge early in the morning to watch the sun burn off the overnight mist. He is a retired vet and has spent his working life caring for animals and, on the river bank, sometimes reflects on the reason why he goes salmon fishing. 'I fish because of the

Guy Hall 'dibbling' on the South Tyne below his house.

challenge, the excitement; I really try to understand the mentality of the salmon. Why it takes a fly is one of the world's great mysteries – they have a mind of their own, even when lying dead on the river bank. Then a salmon takes on a surreal quality, it reminds me of a shark, wild and unpredictable. That's often how I think of myself.

Guy Hall is a member of the Newbrough and Fourstones Angling Club which controls the water below his house. The main towns and villages on the South Tyne – Fourstones, Newbrough, Haydon Bridge, Bardon Mill, Haltwhistle and Alston – all have angling clubs. And from Warden Bridge, just upstream of the meeting of the Tynes, to the bridge at Haydon Bridge there are some famous salmon pools: the Mill pool and race at Warden Paper Mill, the Bend pool, the Limestone pool, the Island pool, Allerwash pool, the Quay wall and the Spa Well pool.

Not all the fishing on the South Tyne is private. At Haydon Bridge the South Tyne Angling Club issues permits for five miles of fishing to anglers staying in the Haydon Bridge area. (The bridge at Haydon Bridge was once the main crossing on the South Tyne and is mentioned in a number of fourteenth-century documents. Like the other bridges on the Tyne it was destroyed by the flood of 1771, and the present bridge dates from 1773.)

From Bardon Mill upstream to Featherstone, the Haltwhistle and District Angling Club leases out six miles of river to visiting anglers, who can also purchase daily or weekly tickets from the Alston and District Angling Association for 12 miles of river between the Lambley Viaduct and the junction of the Black Burn with the South Tyne at Leadgate.

Between Haydon Bridge and Bardon Mill the South Tyne receives its major tributary, the River Allen. About three miles upstream the Allen splits into the East and West Allens. At the top of East Allen Dale is the small town of Allenheads. Half-way down is Allendale Town and here, at the post office, the visiting angler can obtain a permit to fish some six miles of the river from Allenheads down to the Oak pool, just above the confluence of the two Allens, and this stretch of water is stocked with brown trout by the Allendale Angling Association. The two Allens are neither salmon nor sea-trout rivers; the weir at Catton on the East Allen and the weir below Whitfield Hall on the West Allen, with its broken fish pass, block the path of most returning fish. In heavy spates, however, large fish have been seen jumping the weirs, sea trout have been caught in the East Allen, and salmon have sometimes been observed spawning in one of its tributaries, the Acton Burn.

About two miles above the Whitfield weir, the West Allen Burn enters the West Allen. About 500 yards from the banks of the burn, at Middleside, lives one of the worst salmon fishermen of the Tyne. His name is Rod Sutterby. After five years of trying he has yet to land a salmon, although recently he hooked a large one in the South Tyne. He struggled with the fish for half an hour until, to his horror, the line went slack – a swirl, and the fish was gone. Occasionally he catches sea trout, but loses more than he lands. 'I have this bad habit of snagging a tree, in the dark, just before I pack up at night,' he says. 'I tighten up the ratchet on the reel and pull hard to clear the fly; but the cast usually breaks and I lose the fly, and go home feeling disgruntled. The next day I'm on the water again and just after I start fishing, often to my surprise, a large sea trout takes – it's happened on a number of occasions – the fish makes a run, and keeps on running! I've forgotten to slacken off the

OPPOSITE: The Allens just downstream of the confluence of the East and West Allens.

ratchet I tightened the night before, and once more the cast snaps.'

He may catch few fish and he may be an unlucky fisherman, but he is fortunate in other ways. Rod Sutterby has great skill as a painter of fish – 'Now that's how I can best capture them.' Some years ago, in an Alston pub, he casually remarked that he would like to draw a typical, heavy-shouldered Tyne salmon. The next day a fisherman arrived with a 16 lb. 14 oz. cock fish caught at Barhaugh on the South Tyne. It was an interesting fish, not at all typical of the Tyne. It had the tail and mouth of a sea trout with the scale count of a salmon: possibly a salmon–sea trout hybrid. It was a fine specimen and Rod Sutterby painted it; then he decided to paint all the Tyne Waters' game fish.

He takes about a month to paint a fish. The fish must be precisely measured, its proportions calculated, the fin rays and scales accurately counted, and a series of line drawings and washes made before the portrait is completed. (All his fish paintings are authenticated by the Natural History Section of the British Museum.) To date he has painted the Barhaugh hybrid; a springer – a hen fish taken from the main Tyne at Hexham – which weighed 10 lb. and was 29 inches long; and a huge yellow Tyne trout, also taken at Barhaugh, that weighed 4 lb. 8 oz. and was 22½ inches long. Rod Sutterby believes this large trout to be a bull trout similar to those drawn and described by Abel Chapman. Since the East and West Allens are poor salmon and sea-trout rivers he fishes in the South Tyne, usually between Slaggyford and Lambley Viaduct.

This stretch is one of the most beautiful of all the Tyne waters. W. J. Palmer described it in 1882:

The traveller has a choice of ways – an upper road

– the turnpike, which leaves the low road soon after quitting the village [of Slaggyford], the low road keeping near the river, which it crosses by Eals Bridge, and afterwards re-crosses by a wooden bridge, and there is the railway . . . But to see a river well it is needful to find the angler's path, which is by copse and scrub, losing itself now and then on pebbly banks, and through shallow pools and fords, and no one knows the river as your fisherman does, who has 'fished every inch of it', as he will tell you, and, being a lover of nature, as are most toilers of these north county dales, he will soon prove to you that he has an eye for the picturesque as well as for fish in the river. All about Slaggyford are to be seen choice views of the stream, pleasant corners, and quiet reaches reflecting old world backgrounds of moor, and remnants of ancient woodland.

The river has changed little since then, and when George Bolam, naturalist and angler, moved to Upper South Tynedale in 1912 he probably walked the same angler's path.

Bolam settled at Alston for the last phase of his life. He was born in 1859 and died in 1934, six years after the death of his great friend Abel Chapman. When Chapman died he left all his manuscripts to Bolam, to be published or not according to Bolam's wishes: the result was Chapman's *Memories*, published in 1930.

George Bolam kept records of the South Tyne fish that he and others caught, as well as noting down all the animals and plants he observed on the river banks. On 26 July 1918 he recorded that 'Young R. Todd hooked one of 2–3 lbs in the Station pool, Hugh Walton says he saw another splash . . . a poor season tho' plenty of fish up.' He summarised the salmon fishing in 1919 thus: 'No salmon caught in Alston this season. The

only one in the neighbourhood was caught by Tom Gill in Eals Bridge pool on Sept 30th which weighed 16½ lbs.'

The next year, under a heading 'Salmon fishing 1920', Bolam wrote in his diary:

Aug. 6th. Been plenty of small floods, a big one two days ago . . . began season with a whole day, Randalhome to bottom of Kirkhaugh. Sea t. flies – teal and drake and a small one . . . rose a small fish – say 2–3 lbs – just below Kirkhaugh bridge.
Aug. 7th. River almost small again, but good colour. Out after tea . . . to Kirkhaugh over bridge and down E. side. Hooked a 3 pounder in Richardson's pool [200 yards below bridge] but hold gave away after ½ minute. Just after being hooked

he jumped right on to the bank below me, 18″ above water, and rolled in again!
Aug. 9th. Randalholme to Kirkhaugh after tea . . . rose a fish towards 9.30 pm – did not take hold . . . Saw nothing else.

He draws blanks on 10th, 11th, 12th and 19th, but finally:

Aug. 20th. Down . . . after tea and on to roadside pool at dusk when got on a 2 lb 9 oz. – a real Bull trout . . . Teal and claret.
Aug. 21st. River getting low and very cold. Biked to Randalholme and fished down to bottom of pool at Kirkhaugh. Blank sans for one rise in latter – a fish of about 1½ lbs . . . Tom Gill got one

yesterday, about Randalholme, 1½ lbs 'one of the little kind' and another man one of 6 lbs . . . . Sept 4th. Down as far as bottom of Kirkhaugh after tea, good water, blank! I hear Joe Walton has got a small one a week or two ago.

Bolam was not a lucky fisherman. Next year he was on the river bank, rod in hand, almost every day for the first two weeks of August.

13th Aug. I started about 11 and walked down to Randalholme and fished down, here and there, to Lintley pools – dull but fine, a very nice water running in the 'Plain Tree pool' below Kirkhaugh bridge looked so tempting for a 'big fish'. Put on a 'Teal and Yellow' . . . and just at the right spot promptly came a pull! Struck lightly and . . . fish went off with an excellent cast . . . disclosing what I felt certain was a salmon of some 7 or 8 lbs and if so the first I have seen here! . . . It flounced about the pool a good deal ere it quietened down, while a discontented angler sat and smoked a pipe . . . it was my old line which I knew was getting rotten . . . I now snapped off yard after yard of it.

At last, on 16 September 1926, he caught a salmon from the South Tyne. It was a 7-lb. hen fish from the Eals Bridge pool and was 28 inches long.

In the late 1920s, just prior to the years when 'tainted fish' were caught in the polluted estuary, fishing everywhere in the Tyne was excellent. The South Tyne was no exception. In 1927 it was reported that:

Mr R. Allen of Haydon Bridge beat his record of the previous week landing seven salmon, aggregating 110 lbs, his largest fish scaling 23 lbs. There has been an abnormal run of fish up the South Tyne, and the outlook for the remaining six weeks of the season is most promising, as all the pools are now teeming with fish, and many of good size too. (Newcastle Journal, 17 September.)

The estuary died and was reborn, and in 1987 George Bolam's Eals Bridge pool was fishing well again. On 23 August Neil Gillender was fishing Eals for sea trout with a sinking-tip line and 5-lb. cast. It was around five o'clock – he usually starts fishing in the mid-afternoon and continues into the evening – when a powerful fish took the number 10 Black Pennell on his dropper. For over 20 minutes the fish drove up and down the pool. The tail fly, a number 8 Teal and Green, was ripped off before the fish decided to head downstream and run for 300 yards through rough, thin water with Mr Gillender hotly in pursuit and just managing to keep in contact. After 45

A mile below the source of the South Tyne.

minutes the fish finally rolled and came quietly to the bank where it was hand-tailed by a local angler: a 10 lb. 12¼ oz. sea trout. Neil Gillender felt confident of winning the Alston Angling Club's cup for the largest sea trout of the 1987 season. But he didn't; just before the end of the season, Alston angler Derek Nichol caught a fine fish weighing 12 lb. 13¼ oz. It was the second time that Mr Nichol had won the trophy.

Derek Nichol was a founder member of the Alston and District Angling Association. He was born in 1925 in Hexham, and first fished the main Tyne at Tyne Green when he was eight years old. His father and grandfather were both keen Tyne fishermen and he remembers his grandfather fishing for salmon at Hexham with a huge double-handed greenheart rod. His grandfather was a train driver on the Newcastle–Carlisle railway and his father was a guard on the same line. Following the family tradition, Derek joined the railways in 1940. He

worked on the Haltwhistle–Alston branch line as a fireman. He moved to Alston to be nearer his work and has stayed there ever since. He left the railways to work down the local coal pit and, like many miners, went fishing. 'It's being out in the open air away from the dust and dark, close to nature, that's why a lot of us went fishing.' He is certainly close to nature on the Alston beat: deer come down to the water's edge to drink, squirrels leap through the overhanging trees, pheasants strut around the fields and along the river bank scurry an ever-increasing number of wild mink.

Derek Nichol fishes for sea trout with a number 6 Peter Ross fly, both on the tail and the dropper. He uses a 10-foot carbon-fibre rod, a floating line and a 9-foot, 10-lb. breaking-strain cast. He used to fish the Alston club water for brown trout but 'big ones nowadays are few and far between'; nevertheless, trout fishing taught him how to place a line 'quietly and nicely' on the water. He casts across and down at an angle of about 45

The source of the South Tyne.

degrees, and believes concentration and patience are the two best attributes a sea-trout fisherman can have. His favourite pool on the Alston beat is Lintley pool and his 12 lb. 13¼ oz. fish still holds the record for the club's biggest sea trout, although in 1989 the cup-winning fish was just a few ounces less. This magnificent sea trout scaled 12 lb. 8½ oz. at the Alston butcher's shop.

About three miles up-river of Alston is the pretty village of Garrigill where the South Tyne becomes a large stream. The road out of Garrigill, the last village before Tyne Head, travels along the west bank of the river, past the waterfall of the Ashgill Burn which enters the South Tyne on its east bank and into a 'No Through Road.' The road soon becomes a track, one of the many carrier ways that once went to the lead mines. Pack horses, sometimes in groups of 25, carried the lead and ore down from the mines to the smelt and crushing mills long before the arrival of the railways. Small carts were used as well as pack horses, and over the centuries the routes over the fells became well worn and often impassable in stormy weather.

Today the track is rarely used. It is in good condition and follows the banks of the ever-decreasing South Tyne. It is first a small stream and then a tiny clear brook, running over a rocky bottom – but even here sea trout have been known to spawn. The track bridges and rebridges the South Tyne which now has few tributaries and is fed by countless rivulets that run off Tyne Head Fell, Round Hill and Bellbeaver Rigg. The brook itself becomes a tiny rivulet and then disappears, lost in a small patch of marshy peat that is an insignificant part of this high, wide and lonely fell-land.

Salmon spearing from 'trows'.

The Children of Men are deceitful upon the weights.

Psalm 62, Verse 9 – Prayer Book Version.

(Written on the flyleaf of Chipchase Castle
Salmon Book No. 4, 1925)

Chapter 6

THE SOURCE

On North Tyne Head the wind is usually blowing hard and cold. But for once, on top of Windy Knowe, the air is still and barely rustles the silvery grey, wind-flattened clumps of fell grass that point in one direction, like grey waves in a North Sea gale. Today the horizon is hard to see, the grass blending, imperceptibly, into a misty, yellow-grey autumn sky. The few fellside trees are bent and stunted, their trunks knotted and gnarled as they fight to survive harsh winters and poor soil. Moss thrives in this acid, boggy earth; its patches of dark green are the only relief in a lonely beautiful wilderness of grey.

Windy Knowe is in Scotland, and the border with England runs just south of a path that leads half-way up the Knowe from the North Tyne valley to an abandoned quarry and some ruined stone-cutters' cottages. The border follows Bells Burn which runs into the North Tyne, south of Bells Moor. These fells and valleys were fought over by Scotland and England for three centuries before the Union. In order to control and administer the border area during this period it was broken up into regions or 'marches' – the East, Middle and West Marches – and Scottish and English 'Wardens of the Marches' were responsible to their respective crowns for settling disputes and maintaining law and order. But this was often very difficult. Henry VIII, for example, actively encouraged the border clans to raid, even

ordering the Duke of Northumberland 'to let slip them of Tynedale and Redesdale for the annoyance of Scotland' and instructing Sir William Percy 'to make a raid at least once a week while the grass is on the ground' (Watson). It was not surprising that the border clansmen lived and acted outside the law, as poverty and hunger forced them to raid and plunder. (In Tynedale, because of the ancient law of gavelkind, the land was continually being subdivided into plots that were too small to support a family. Gavelkind ruled that farmland had to be divided equally between a father's sons.) It is almost certain that the border men took salmon from the small streams where the returning fish made their redds. But this was a seasonal, unsure source of food and both Scottish and English clansmen went plundering or 'reiving' across the border for cattle, sheep and horses. In the sixteenth century, when Tynedale reivers were most active, kinship groups, like the Robsons, Charltons, Milburns and Dodds, were never far from horse, sword and lance. Reivers were sometimes caught by the warden's men, and Bells Kirk, near Deadwater, was a traditional meeting place where the Scottish and English wardens met to exchange captives, deal with those who had broken the laws of the marches and settle border disputes. The border laws were harsh. Englishmen were hung for helping Scottish reivers, or for the crime of marrying Scottish women without the English warden's consent. (Charlton, *Upper North Tynedale*).

Today the valley is emptier and quieter. The Victorian railway that once served this region has gone, and Tyneside's industrial revolution has depopulated much of this part of the North Tyne valley. But some families stayed. The Halls continue to work Deadwater Farm, near a bridge over the Deadwater Burn.

Deadwater Burn rises on Peel Fell that towers over Windy Knowe on the other side of the valley, and some think that this is the source of the River Tyne. 'But it's not, it's here,' said Robert Hall. He had shown us a small water-filled hollow down in the valley a few hours before we had walked up Windy Knowe. 'That's the source of the Tyne. It's strange as I've never seen a spring, but there's always water here, even during the driest summers. Not that we get many of those. I was shown it by my father.'

The fishing rights on both sides of the river from the source of Tyne Waters to the junction of the North Tyne with the Lewis Burn, which now flows into Kielder Reservoir, have traditionally been owned by the dukes of Northumberland. At one time Deadwater farm also belonged to the dukes, but when the eighth duke died in 1930 much of the land was sold to the Forestry Commission to raise money to pay death duties. Today the Halls work nearly 1500 acres of Forestry Commission land. They have some 900 sheep, Swaledale ewes and Hereford crosses, and Robert Hall's younger brother James is the shepherd. He has spent most of his life on the fells, his only company his sheep dogs. In April, during the lambing season, he rises at four each morning and at first light can be seen disappearing up Bells Moor, his rolling gait and wide stride carrying him over more than 15 miles of fells each day. He used to see salmon and sea trout in the small burns of these fells before Kielder Dam was built and blocked the path of the returning fish. In one 'shaley-bottomed sike' he saw spawning salmon every year, and once saw a cock fish of around 20 lb. 'It was so big that it could hardly turn round, but somehow it found a mate, and it bred!'

According to the Halls, the source of the River Tyne lies just on the English side of the border

with Scotland, in a field north of the road, about half a mile from Deadwater Burn which is 'not the source, but the Tyne's first major tributary'. In 1882 W. J. Palmer placed the source of the Tyne 'within the enclosure of the North British Railway . . . near some old stone-cutting sheds connected with a quarry seen on the Fell side, and some yards beyond a sulphur well which here marks the Border'. The sulphur well was 'much frequented by persons suffering from scrofulous complaints, and only wants proper accommodation to make it a place of greater resort . . . Old inhabitants speak to having seen many years since round the spot, a cluster of wooden houses for bathing, &c., but these have disappeared long since.'

In the 1930s, as a boy, Robert Hall drank from the sulphur spring. In 1989 it was destroyed when

James Hall near the source of the North Tyne. The road crosses the trackway of the old Border counties railway.

a powerful Forestry Commission plough went right through it, exposing a few broken pieces of china, some thickly glazed green bottles and a few waterlogged timbers – the last remnants, perhaps, of the old bathing huts.

Growing up in the 1930s the Hall brothers fished the North Tyne for salmon, sea trout, brownies and 'anything else we could catch' with bamboo rods and worms. The river flows sluggishly, now as it did then, through a peaty, boggy valley, and is fed by countless small streams – 'grains, sikes and burns'. Palmer's description of the North Tyne as 'a silver thread in a channel of peat as black as night' is still apt. The valley floor is so marshy that in order to bring the railway to this part of Tyne Head the track's foundations were first laid on bundles of local sheep's wool which were then packed hard into the wet ground with hardcore and gravel.

The railway was used by all the local hill farmers, including three generations of the Halls of Deadwater, to carry their sheep to Bellingham market. The line also carried limestone and freestone – perhaps from worked-out Deadwater quarry – and coal, possibly from the defunct Plashetts mine, down to Tyneside. Deadwater Station, almost opposite Deadwater Farm, still exists but in 1956 the North Tyne line was axed and the iron rails were lifted; the grass-covered trackway can still be seen. The end came almost 100 years after William Henry Charlton ceremonially drove a spade into the ground just outside Hexham to inaugurate the line in 1855. In the previous year an Act of Parliament had created a 'Border Counties Railway' and a significant portion of the funding came from local landed gentry, such as the Duke of Northumberland, the Charltons of Hesleyside and the Beaumonts of Bywell. By 1862 the North British Railway Company had completed a single-line track which ran from Hexham up the North Tyne valley and linked with the Carlisle–Hawick–Edinburgh line at Riccarton on the River Liddel in Scotland.

The station below Deadwater was Tarset and then came Kielder, situated not far from Kielder Castle – a shooting lodge built in 1775 by the Duke of Northumberland for his North Tyne Estate. Near Kielder a beautiful high-arched viaduct was built to carry the track across the North Tyne, and it now stands in 5 feet of water at the head of Bakethin Reservoir. It is possible that the sea trout released into the Bakethin Reservoir by Gordon Earsman will spawn in the sikes and burns of North Tyne Head; perhaps their young will return to the sea by crossing the watershed and entering a small feeder stream of the River Liddel that eventually runs into the Solway Firth. In 1989 an angler took a sea trout weighing nearly 4 lb. from Bakethin Reservoir.

The railway track can still be seen along the north side of Bakethin Reservoir, but Kielder Reservoir covers most of the stretch that once ran between the next two stations down the valley, Plashetts and Falstone. The Duke of Northumberland owned the fishing rights on the north banks of the Tyne down from Lewis Burn to Plashetts Station. He kept for his own use the fishing upstream of Plashetts Station, but did allow visiting anglers to fish a four-mile stretch downstream of the station.

In 1851 two gamekeepers were given permission to mine for coal at Plashetts provided they supplied the Duke's hunting lodge at Kielder. This was the beginning of the Plashetts Colliery, and the mine was one of the major reasons why the Duke of Northumberland supported the building of the railway up the North Tyne valley. The colliery was situated near Belling Burn and a village aptly named 'Seldom Seen' was built to house the miners. The mine, abandoned by the 1930s, was leased out by the Duke of Northumberland in 1889. He made a stipulation that the lessees must not employ anyone 'known to be game or fish poachers, and in the event of any workman or workmen becoming a nuisance to the estate through improper trespass in search of game or fish then the lessee undertakes to dismiss the offending parties'. The local landowners (then and now) saw salmon fishing not only as a means of recreation but also as an asset and a possible source of income from visiting sportsmen. When the Hawkhope Estate near Falstone was put up for sale in 1867 the advertisement read, 'The District is famous for grouse and black game [black grouse] while excellent salmon and trout fishing are available in the North Tyne which forms one mile of the estate boundary.' To protect their interests the landowners had, as early as 1834, formed a North Tyne and Reedwater Association for the Prevention of Poaching (Charlton, *Upper North Tynedale*).

In the early part of the nineteenth century Falstone was the last village in the North Tyne valley before the fells and moors of Upper Tynedale, and was the base for visiting anglers and walkers. In 1835 William Andrew Chatto (under the pseudonym of Stephen Oliver the Younger; see Bibliography) wrote, in *Rambles in Northumberland*: 'At Falstone there is an excellent public house, and only one, the "Black Cock" . . . which, though only a cottage, affords to the angler in summer and the shooter in autumn better accommodation than many an inn of greater pretensions.' But there was no public house beyond Falstone in North Tynedale, 'and the tourist who intends to proceed towards Tyne-head, and to pass over the hills into Scotland, will do well to replenish his flask and provide

himself with a two days' supply of solids.'

In 1882, when W. J. Palmer was writing and the railway line was open, the Black Cock was still taking care of anglers:

Falstone affords the best head-quarters when making excursions in Upper Tynedale. The 'Black Cock' is the sign of the comfortable inn close to the church. The sign is the same as that of the house concerning which Stephen Oliver the Younger wrote so genially some forty years ago. But few old fashioned characteristics are to be found in the new 'Black Cock', built on the site of the old one ten years ago . . . Fishers and shooters are her most considerable customers, the summer months otherwise bringing but occasional visitors to this little-known district. (Palmer.)

The Black Cock nowadays has many visitors, often those on their way to enjoy the water sports, which include trout fishing, on Kielder Reservoir. It continues to help visiting anglers by supplying permits, issued by the Falstone Fishing Club, to fish for salmon on a two-mile stretch of the North Tyne.

Falstone village is about a mile away from the huge 170-foot-high Kielder Dam that young Jonathan Hall of Deadwater Farm officially closed in December 1979. Released dam water generates electricity by hydroelectric power as it pours into the North Tyne. It rises high in the air as it leaves the face of the dam – twin jets of foaming white water. Some anglers claim that because the released water comes from deep in the reservoir it lacks oxygen and is detrimental to river life, but in all probability the water is rapidly reoxygenated as it passes out of the dam and tumbles down the North Tyne valley. A second complaint from anglers is that released water is at a different temperature from that of the river. This might, for example, prevent young parr from coming on to feed if the water temperature is below the critical temperature of 7°C. However, it is likely that these temperature differences only affect the redds within a mile or two of the dam face. The Kielder hatchery also makes up any losses by removing adult salmon from this part of the river, using them in its artificial breeding programme, and restocking this part of the North Tyne with 'mature' parr. A third complaint is that sudden releases of reservoir water are dangerous to wading anglers. But this is nothing new, as the North Tyne was always prone to sudden floods. In 1904 Augustus Grimble wrote that the North Tyne

> is subject to sudden spates and very quick rises, so the angler must keep his eyes open for indications of water rush, or he may find himself in a fix; sharp eyes will usually detect small sticks and leaves come floating by; under such circumstances any one who is wading deep will do well to make for the bank and watch events for a short time.

There is still much evidence on the north bank of the river of the old railway line between Falstone and its next station down the valley, Bellingham. In 1834 Bellingham was, according to Chatto/Oliver, 'the most considerable village on North Tyne. It consists of about seventy houses, mostly built of and covered with stone . . .', and it was here that he met with the salmon 'trows'. 'I noticed at Bellingham, as well as at two other places up North Tyne, a curious sort of double boat, called by the country people "the trows", which is used in spearing salmon in parts of the river where they cannot be taken with a net.' The trows were like two narrow boats joined at the bow and stern:

> Each single boat is flat-bottomed; about ten feet long; fourteen inches deep . . . They are formed of deal, and are extremely slight . . . In spearing

salmon from those trows, there are usually two men in each; one to guide them by means of a long pole, called a 'bang', and the other armed with a leister, to look out for and strike the fish. The man who guides the boat is stationed towards the stern, while he who has the leister stands with one leg in each trow looking down into the water between them, and on each side, in order to see if there be any salmon. If the trow happens to pass directly over the place where a fish lies, he strikes down between them; and, according to the place in which he perceives a salmon, he also strikes over the stem or on each side.

A net was often placed at the head of a pool to prevent the salmon from leaving, and after the fish first appeared in a pool the trows were pushed around for a few days in order to accustom the fish to them.

> Some of the old trow-fishers here are of the opinion, that if the hearing of the salmon were as good as their sight, there would be no killing them with leister in daylight. The trows are only used in the season when salmon may be legally taken, and in daylight; though perhaps they may now and then be used in the dark, with a wisp burning in the stem; for some of the people of Bellingham have the character of being great poachers, both of fish and fowl, spearing salmon in close time and killing the grouse, which abound on neighbouring moors, without asking the owner's leave.

Chatto was a keen angler and recounts how one day, out fishing, he met an old Bellingham poacher who described 'his "leistering" adventures in triumphant glee'. With nine other Bellingham poachers and four horses they had set out one night to poach the River Coquet. Eight waded into the river, six with leisters and two with lights, while two men stayed on the bank, one on each side of the river, to keep a look-out. But they were surprised by the local gamekeepers or 'watchers' and 'ever sae many chaps from Rothbury'. The Bellingham poachers were asked to give themselves up, but they refused and stayed put, forcing the watchers and their men to come at them in the river. A terrible fight followed, 'they makin' at us wi' sticks, and we layin' on like mad wi' the leisters'. The two sides fought, rolling over and over in the water just like

Auld John Walker and auld Jin Sim,
He ower her, and she ower him.

But the watchers and Rothbury men had no chance, for 'we were a' great strang fellows, fighting like perfect deevils for our salmon, and for fear o' Morpeth gaol'. The Bellingham men got clear and rode home, and just before Bellingham they 'parted the salmon on the hill head; and A! it was a bonny seet to see them, for there was mare than a hundred, great and sma', lyin' on the grass i' the first glint o' the mornin''.

Chatto fished the North Tyne some three years after the Bywell weir was lowered and in his time salmon and grilse were increasingly being taking on the fly near Bellingham. In those days grilse arrived at this stretch around the first week in July, and salmon about a month later.

Fifty years later Palmer visited the same stretch of the North Tyne and wrote about trow fishing with leisters as a thing of the past. 'In the neighbourhood of Bellingham and higher up the river where salmon cannot be taken with the net, spearing from a boat was formerly a common practice.' He described the word 'leister' as being derived from the Danish 'lyster' or Icelandic 'ljoster', both words meaning 'a barbed iron fork on a long pole', and 'trow' as derived from a Jutland word for a small river ferry that was

originally two hollowed-out tree trunks joined together by a cross-pole. The occupant placed a foot in the trough of each tree-trunk boat and propelled it with an oar or pole.

In present-day Bellingham a large stone-built house accommodates the Riverdale Hall Hotel. Every year salmon are taken from the hotel's water where fishing is free for residents. If a guest is lucky enough to catch a salmon it may be cooked by Iben Broust-Cocker, resident chef and wife of the proprietor John Cocker. She knows all about the derivation of the word 'leister' as she comes from Copenhagen.

About a mile and a half downstream from Bellingham the North Tyne receives its largest tributary, the River Rede (occasionally spelt Reed). The old North British Railway line bridged the Rede just north of Redesmouth House and there was a station at Redesmouth where the line branched. A Wansbeck section of the line went east, following the south bank of the Rede for some miles; its grass-covered trackway is still in evidence.

The Wansbeck branch line left the Rede valley near the Roman fort at Habitancum. The fort once guarded the river crossing of Dere Street, the important Roman road that went from Corbridge up to the major Roman base of Newstead in Scotland. Dere Street recrossed the River Rede near a fort at Blakehope, and travelled up the valley to another fort at High Rochester (Bremenium) before passing along the banks of Sills Burn and out of the valley. Both Habitancum and Bremenium were important posts; at one time each housed 1000 cavalry as well as units of mounted scouts. Bremenium means 'the place of the roaring stream', which must refer to nearby Sill Burn when it was in full flood.

Dere Street became the western boundary of

the kingdom of Northumbria that was created after the Angles invaded the east coast, and for centuries it was the main route into Scotland until the turnpike roads were constructed in the eighteenth and nineteenth centuries. But long before the turnpikes Redesdale was criss-crossed with a network of minor farm roads, fell paths, border paths and Scottish drovers' tracks. The drovers brought sheep and cattle down the valley to what was then the most important town in Redesdale, Elsdon.

Redesdale, like upper North Tynedale, has had a violent history. When the kingdom of Northumbria fell, Anglo-Scottish conflicts raged up and down the valley. To defend the border against the Scots Redesdale was designated a special area or 'liberty', directly under the English king's authority. William the Conqueror gave the liberty to his cousin, Robert Umphraville, Lord of Redesdale, who had to supply men and arms for its defence; but in return the Lords of Redesdale claimed many privileges. One was the right to claim a tax (supposedly only paid by Scotsmen!) for the river crossing at Elishaw, near the Roman fort at Blakehope.

Redeswire, not far from the source of the River Rede, was the site of the 'Redeswire fray'. In the sixteenth century reivers were very active; probably even more so than those of Upper Tynedale. In 1575 there was a 'day of law' when the Warden of the English Middle Marches met his Scottish counterpart at Redeswire. After much heavy drinking, however, feuding broke out between different clansmen, Scots and Englishmen, and many were killed including the English deputy warden. In an attempt to suppress reiving and restore order, special watches were kept over all the fords on the River Rede, but it was not until the Union of Scotland and England that brigandage came to an end.

In the early sixteenth century Otterburn Tower was owned by the Halls, who had succeeded the Umphravilles. One of this family, 'Mad Jack' Hall, supported the unsuccessful 1715 Jacobite rebellion. He was captured and taken to London, where he was hung, drawn and quartered at Tyburn. It is said by the present proprietors of the Otterburn Towers, now a hotel, that his ghost haunts the tower.

Today the Otterburn Towers Hotel owns, and issues permits for, a 3½-mile stretch of the north bank of the River Rede. The beat runs south of Mill Bridge, the fishing is free to residents, and the hotel has good sea-trout and salmon runs – sometimes in February but more usually in September and October, providing there has been a number of reasonably heavy spates. In 1987 a 30-lb. fresh-run salmon was taken from the hotel's water, and all the salmon and sea trout served by the Otterburn Towers restaurant have been obtained from the hotel's beat by local anglers.

One of the hotel's postmen is a keen fisher of the beat. Each morning until recently, the mail was brought up to the village by van from Newcastle, but the postmen had to wait until three o'clock in the afternoon before returning with the post. Although the post office supplied a rest room, 'Postman John' preferred to spend his time fishing. He not only returned to Newcastle with the mail, but more often than not with a few 'brownies' and, if he was lucky, a sea trout or a salmon.

Opposite the Otterburn Towers is another hotel, the Percy Arms. Its origins lie in the eighteenth century when drovers stopped at a tiny inn near the bridge over the Otter Burn. The drovers' track became the Redesdale turnpike, and in the early nineteenth century the inn became a staging post for the London–Edinburgh passenger and mail coaches. Today it serves

travellers on a major road into Scotland. An infamous member of its more recent clientele was 'Sally the Mugger' who 'was a mighty woman of Herculean build who hawked cartloads of poached salmon around the district each autumn' (Charlton, *The Story of Redesdale*). Nowadays there is no need to poach the Rede as the Percy Arms leases a mile and a half of salmon fishing, free to residents, on the north bank of the river upstream of the Mill Bridge.

Occasional catches are made in the River Rede of rainbow trout that have probably escaped from the stocked Catcleugh Reservoir at Rede Head. (Catcleugh was apparently named after the wildcats that once roamed the little gullies or 'cleughs' in the valley sides.) The reservoir was completed in 1905 by the Newcastle and Gateshead Water Company to supply the population of a rapidly expanding Tyneside. Unlike Kielder Reservoir it was dug out mainly by

pick and shovel, although a 'Ruston steam excavator' – much distrusted by the men – was also employed. A special hutted village was built to contain the 500 or so labourers who came from Tyneside to build the reservoir, and a narrow-gauge railway was built to carry men and materials from the branch-line station at Woodburn to Catcleugh.

An Act of Parliament was passed in 1889 allowing the Newcastle and Gateshead Water Company to construct a small reservoir at Catcleugh on condition that a fish pass was built for the returning salmon. The directors offered to make a payment of £3850 to the Fishery Department of the Board of Trade to be excused from building the pass, and when their offer was accepted the company promoted a new parliamentary bill for the building of the reservoir, this time omitting the clause making obligatory the construction of the fish pass. For

The outlet of the Catcleugh reservoir at the head of the River Rede.

technical reasons the bill was not successful, but by then it had been decided to build a larger reservoir; now, the directors argued, the height of the dam face would make a fish pass impossible. A new Act was passed for the larger reservoir, the fish pass was abandoned, and the Fishery Department got £3850. The Newcastle and Gateshead Water Company's only obligation was to supply gratings to prevent fish from leaving the reservoir. There was also an optimistic recommendation that, as salmon spawning 'could not now take place, improvements benefiting fisheries should be made elsewhere on the Tyne' (Rennison). In 1905, as the waters began to rise, the reservoir was stocked with fish and the water company joined with the Duke of Northumberland to form an angling club that still exists.

The reservoir is a monument to Victorian engineering: today the stonework is as solid and sound as when it was first built. Pump house, walls, dam and arches have a cathedral-like quality, and the bed of the overspill has the appearance of a newly built Roman road. The Victorian engineers built a pipeline to take water to Colt Crag and Whittle Dene reservoirs, which in turn supplied Tyneside. Initially the pipe was cleaned by sending gangs of six to eight men down it. They would lie on their backs, on trolleys, and by candle-light scrape off the rust and mud. This filthy mixture was loaded into buckets and manhandled out of the pipe; the cleaning used to take 120 men two weeks. In 1943 a simpler method was introduced. A small section of the pipe was unbolted and a tightly fitting circular brush pushed inside the pipe. The section was replaced and the brush, blown along by water pressure, scoured the insides of the pipe clean in a couple of days.

In times of drought, releases of water from

Catcleugh Reservoir can be used to flush out the Rede but its 2.4 million-gallon capacity is very small compared to the 233 million-gallon capacity of the Kielder Reservoir that feeds the North Tyne. In the hot summer of 1989 the River Rede was almost reduced to a trickle, and the river fished badly until the spates of very late autumn when only a few salmon were taken. The water released from Kielder kept the North Tyne above drought levels and the river relatively free from algal growth, and salmon were caught in August and September. The Rede, being a small, remote river, has always been easy to poach, which is one reason why it fishes less well than the North Tyne!

Sir Herbert Maxwell, author of *Salmon and Sea Trout*, describes a frustrating day's fishing on this part of the North Tyne in 1867.

I had come some miles by train to Reedsmouth Station, whence I walked down to the Hargroves water. I was alone. I had not brought my gaff, and the river was very heavy, but I soon got among fish, and landed eight salmon and two grilse, weighing in all 90 lbs – nothing above 13 lbs. Each fish had to be towed ashore and tailed out, which is apt to be severe on the rod. It proved so in this case, for I broke my only top three times, and had to sit down and repair it twice: the third time darkness closed upon the scene. Oh, the precious moments wasted! Oh, the trembling fingers that bound the twine of sandwich papers so clumsily round the fractures! Oh, the want of foresight or the laziness that made me bring out only one rod!

Five years later, in the autumn of 1872, Maxwell again took the train to Redesmouth. This time he was well prepared:

The most rapid and unflagging sport I ever had . . . I killed 46 salmon and grilse weighing 561 lbs.

in four days and a half. The forty-sixth fish was hooked with the last cast on the fifth day. I had no more than time to land him, and run up to Reedsmouth Station to catch the 1 P.M. train. Papae! how often I have groaned over the engagement that took me to Edinburgh when fish were in such a glorious mood! That fifth day was the only one on which I have known salmon to rise well in a thick fog. Generally it may be regarded as the one aspect of meteorology fatal to sport; yet on this occasion between 10 A.M. and 12.30 I landed six salmon weighing 88½ lbs. (largest fish 21 lbs.), and had I been able to finish the day I must have achieved an average for the five days of over ten fish a day. Such chances do not occur often in an angler's lifetime.

Fishing, a strange and haunting pastime, has always attracted eccentric and wonderful characters. Maxwell described one.

At Reedsmouth, the junction of the Reed and the North Tyne, there lived, in the days I speak of, a certain Dr Begg, who rented the fishing of a couple of casts on the main river . . . the worthy doctor could not have measured more than five feet in his stocking soles. When I first met him, early in October, 1867, he had killed upwards of 150 salmon and grilse with the fly during that season. And such flies! all of nearly the same pattern – fat, fuzzy bodies, generally of gray rabbit or monkey wool, enormously over-winged, on small single hooks – and nearly all of the same size, rather large, and tied on collars of undyed treble gut . . . He would get into a pair of enormous wading trousers, button his long, yellow 'Piccadilly weeper' whiskers into his coat, clap on a cowboy hat, stuck all over with hairy salmon flies, take his spliced rod, of the Castle Connel type, off the rack, and stroll down to the river. Wading in almost to the armpits, he would begin on a fine stream which ran at the

foot of his garden, ever since known as the Doctor's stream, flinging his flies (he always used two of these monstrosities at once) across the current at right angles and bringing them round to within a few yards of where he was standing. No low point and deep fly with him! On the contrary, he gradually raised the point of his rod after delivering the cast, trailing the flies along the surface of the water, so that when he had finished the circuit his rod was quite erect . . .

Kindly, quaint, 'Brownie of the Tyne', as we used to call him . . . many a time do I recall his extraordinary appearance – a huge hat, a very red face, and a pair of arms emerging from the expanse of gleaming brown water; and as often do I reflect with gratitude on his readiness – so rare among anglers – to let a friend fish the best of the water before him. His prodigious whiskers landed him in a painful dilemma once. He had hooked a strong fish in mid-stream, and was making his way ashore, with rod held aloft to keep it clear of the water. His whiskers had been snugly housed and buttoned down as usual when he started, but a button having given way, one of them had escaped and fluttered in the breeze. It caught in the revolving handle of the reel, for the salmon was running merrily, and was wound up tightly to his cheek. He managed to land his fish, but the whisker had to be shorn off close before he was released.

Maxwell described another fishing incident on this stretch of water when, in *Post Meridiana: Afternoon Essays* (1895), he wrote about one of his 'most cherished idols':

a salmon-fly – a double-hooked Childers – which I tied wellnigh a quarter of a century ago. With this fly I began fishing in the Hargroves water on the North Tyne one September morning. A fish rolled up at the fly, was held for a moment, and the gut snapped. The salmon was free. Next day there was

TOP: *The tail of the Diagonal Pool, Countess Park.*
BOTTOM: *Houxty Burn.*

a small flood and no fishing; but on the third day the river was again in trim. My companion began fishing half a mile or so above where I had met the mishap. When we met for lunch, he showed me a fly which he had found fixed in the breast of the fish he had landed. It was my lost Childers. I put it on, and killed two salmon with it the same afternoon.

The Hargroves beat was just below Redesmouth and, before pollution struck the lower reaches, this and further downstream sections of the river produced some of the Tyne Waters' finest angling – and record salmon. The Lee Hall water commenced just below Countess Park and ran downstream for about two miles. This beat produced some fine catches. Augustus Grimble, writing in 1913, described the water in some detail; it has changed little since then.

Seven principal pools or streams, all of which have to be waded with trousers or boated; commencing at the top of the water The Heugh comes first, a broad pool some quarter of a mile in length and in parts twenty feet deep, with high and picturesque cliffs. Then comes the Devil's Leap, with very good streams at the head of it, and when in good ply some parts of it are close to fifty feet deep. The Upper Dovecote follows, good on both sides, with a nice rising depth of water throughout. The Lower Dovecote is a short but good cast; then passing Lee Hall, are the Halfway House, the Ash Trees and the Mill Stream, which is the best of these three casts and is quite one hundred and fifty yards long with a nice rising depth of water . . . The rods used vary from fifteen to eighteen feet, according to the time of year . . . Salmon average about 14 lb and grilse 5 lb; sea trout are rare and weigh from 2 to 3 lb, the best ever got here scaled 4 lb; bull trout are numerous and average 4 lb with occasionally one going up to 8 lb; the heaviest recorded scaled 10 lb.

It was Colonel Fife Cookson who had the best bag when on 6 October 1885 he caught five salmon, 15 grilse and five bull trout. The heaviest fish on this beat was taken by Sir Aubone Fife on 17 October 1892 – a 32-lb. salmon from the head of the Devil's Leap pool. Writing about this stretch of water in 1908, A. G. Bradley described it as a:

broad and lusty river with the dark hue of peat moss just tinging its clear streams, [that] sweeps out of the Duke's wood [Countess Park] below the confluence of the Rede, and curves finely round the meadows below the house; while the Houxty burn, a lusty stream from the moors, comes pouring down through pine woods beside it. There is no doubt about the salmon in the North Tyne, two or three favourite pools, within sight of the windows, yield their annual tribute; and indeed, for twenty odd miles up from its mouth at Warden, to Falstone, beyond Bellingham, the salmon fishing is everywhere excellent when the water is right. The bull trout too, the salmo eriox, running sometimes to five or six pounds, or even more, loves the North Tyne . . .

Just south of the point where the Houxty Burn enters the Tyne lived another of the Tyne's famous men, Abel Chapman, author of *Bird-Life of the Borders* and 'well known as a naturalist, sportsman, wild-fowler and big-game hunter . . . seated in a house full of trophies from lands remote' (Bradley).

Abel Chapman was one of those great Victorian hunter/naturalists whose delight, according to his friend and fellow naturalist George Bolam, 'lay as much in studying their quarry in life as in bringing it to hand'.

He was born in 1851 at Silksworth Hall, Sunderland, the eldest son of a prosperous brewer. He became a passionate and resourceful traveller,

Spanish ibex from extinction, discovering the main European breeding grounds of the flamingo, elucidating the snow-burrowing habits of grouse and the plumage phases and migration patterns of some waders (Bolam). He was also one of the first, along with Herbert Maxwell, to observe that salmon do not feed in fresh water. In his book *Wild Norway* he wrote:

> *If there are those who still hold that salmon 'feed' while in fresh water, let them consider what that hypothesis involves. Salmon ascend favourite streams in shoals; they are by nature rapacious and voracious – their build and equipment show this, as well as the rapidity with which they recover condition and put on flesh at sea. What is there in any river to satisfy hundreds of such appetites? If they required to be so satisfied, a single week's ravages would clear out every living thing in the water . . . every trout, smolt, or eel, every duck, moor-hen and water-rat, would speedily be swept up – in a week small boys would hardly be safe.*

a talented artist and writer, a fanatical birdwatcher and naturalist, and a keen, indeed obsessive angler. Having divested himself of responsibility for the family business in 1897, he quickly purchased the Houxty Estate on the banks of the North Tyne and spent the next 30 years building, planting and creating a natural sanctuary for 'all kinds of wild things'.

Abel Chapman's travels took him from the Arctic to the Equator. He was the author of ten books in which he enthusiastically described, and delicately drew, hundreds of exotic wild beasts and birds. His intention was always to reach 'the average reader who possesses some love for the "outbye" country and its bird-life in their wilder aspects'. He was a hunter but also contributed much to the preservation and understanding of wildlife, creating the Sabi Game Reserve or Kruger National Park in South Africa, saving the

Chapman had a healthy disregard for purely academic science, which 'so far from advancing knowledge, on occasion is apt to poison its fountain heads by persistently continuing to support . . . some theory or other that has already been shown to be untenable by those few who have enjoyed the opportunity of testing its credibility in the field'. He was one of a 'Band of thoughtful and observant Naturalists, who view the antics of their ill-ballasted brethren with equal sorrow and silence. These silent ranks, moreover, are mainly recruited from those venturesome spirits – from men whose lives have largely been spent in the outer wilderness where man stands face to face with Wild-Life by day and by night, and learns his lessons at first-hand.'

Many of Chapman's best drawings and studies of wildlife were carried out near home: the salmon

Abel Chapman, just before his death in 1929.

and sea trout of the Houxty Burn and the North Tyne, and the birds of Northumberland's sea-shore and fells.

Through his books, *Bird Life of the Borders, Memories of Fourscore Years less Two, Wild Norway* and *The Borders and Beyond*, it is possible to recreate the angler's season as well as the life history of North Tyne salmon and sea trout. As a fisherman, Chapman's pet hates were the spawned salmon, or kelts, that stayed in the river until early spring: 'The salmon kelt . . . Dear old friend! Could I ever be brought to *detest* any one of God's creatures, truly it would be *YOU!*' He recognised their worth for the future salmon stocks of the Tyne but became incensed by the way they took his trout flies during the months of March, April and early May, when North Tyne trout fishing was at its best. Small by comparison with those of the southern chalk streams, a 'large' Border 'brownie' weighed a pound. Chapman's largest was caught at Houxty on 23 May 1906 and weighed 2¾ lb. and was 21 inches long. Brown trout rises in March might last for just minutes, in April an hour, perhaps two, and rises always occurred between eleven and three o'clock. It was during these frequent rises that Chapman dreaded the 'sullen pull' of a salmon kelt seizing his Teal and Yellow. He described how the trout continued to rise all around him in 'tantalising security' as his 12-foot rod and fine tackle played out the kelt for some 20 minutes before it was landed and the fly removed from its 'uninvited and undesired jaws'. Before the 1914–18 war when men were available to act as gillies, Chapman went trout fishing with two rods. When a kelt struck during a rise he would pick up the second rod and continue trouting, while 'the keeper then did the needful for friend kelt'!

One fine April day, while trout fishing, 'something big' seized his tail fly and he assumed

that his captive 'was one more unwelcome kelt'. But he was wrong – a fresh-run spring salmon had taken his fly. He fought the fish for 40 minutes, unable to land it with his light trout tackle. Finally the salmon, in a desperate run, stripped off 38 of his 40 yards of line and Chapman had no choice but to check the line and risk 'a smash'. Feeling the restraint the salmon leapt clear out of the pool, but somehow managed to hook the top fly into the root of the tail. This worked to Chapman's advantage for at once the fish became docile, its tail held upstream and its head downstream, and he was able to land a fine 7¼-lb. cock salmon. Later the same day, he caught 'a pretty hen salmon of 5¼ lb' casting to the same lie but this time with suitable gear – 'so I had a great April day!' (In autumn Chapman sometimes took pairs of salmon, 'one after the other, at precisely the same spot and perhaps an hour later – the second being of the opposite sex'.)

Writing with a fine Victorian style he complained about the kelts:

When in March, each upland rill and rivulet swells to a torrent – when the brown slopes of the moor are streaked and seamed with snow-white cascades: when Houxty burn waxes to the verisimilitude of a river – and torrential at that – when North Tyne, carrying the overflow of a thousand hills, thunders past in tearing flood, a dozen feet above its normal level – at such times one might reasonably expect the poor sea-hungry kelts to seize with both hands – or rather fins – the proffered opportunity to regain the tide . . . but they do not go . . . Only quite exceptionally and after winters of continuous rainfall . . . are our rivers clear of kelts before the end of April.

The latest he ever saw a kelt was on 11 May, and the largest dead kelt he recorded was 44½ inches long with a 20-inch girth. It weighed 21 lb. and Chapman estimated its fresh-run weight to be 37 or 38 lb. Once, on 7 May 1918, under Wark Bridge, he saw salmon both ascending and descending the river. The river was running hard with a 2-foot flood, and some springers were 'splashing up-stream with a wake like that of a destroyer', while kelts were dropping downstream – tail first.

Springers usually arrived at Houxty around February and March. Exceptionally, fish were caught in the Lee Hall water above Houxty in late February, and Thomas Taylor of Chipchase Castle, downstream of Houxty, regularly caught fish in February provided conditions were right – namely if there was a succession of big floods.

Chapman started salmon fishing in late April and continued into May when 'every fair-sized flood will bring up fresh spring salmon'. A few salmon ran in June and July, but generally the summer months produced few fish; however July was 'bull-trout' and grilse month. The Northumberland bull trout was classified by the Victorians as *Salmo eriox*, but now all trout, whether migratory or non-migratory, have been reclassified as *Salmo trutta*. Chapman had his own views about classification: 'The Bull-Trout . . . whatever its scientific status, is the fish recognised under that name by every angler on North Tyne and Redewater,' and in *The Borders and Beyond* he gives sketches showing the difference between sea and bull trout and argues (incorrectly) that 'the true sea-trout is of extremely rare occurrence in North Tyne . . .'

Chapman's bull trout (3–6-lb. sea trout) would arrive in the North Tyne in July when, according to a local saying, 'the alder leaf is as big as a bull's eye'. The bull trout's arrival would be delayed by lack of spates but even a small rise of water, as little as six inches, would bring the fish up to

Houxty. Then they readily took the fly, 'A medium sized sea-trout fly (Teal-and-Yellow in particular, they seem unable to resist!)'.

Tyne bull-trout fishing was best in the evening when, wrote Chapman, 'lingering twilight slowly fades, yet hardly disappears; while waning colours softly change on the moss-brown streams till detail is lost and one is only conscious of the murmur of those swirling waters. The line one can no longer see, and only judges the position of the gently-working lures by a sort of instinct.' A 4-lb. fresh-run bull trout took a 'Dark-Teal-and-Purple' and on such evenings 'you may linger till past ten o'clock, and dine towards midnight'. On such an evening Capt. A. G. Allgood, fishing at Blindburn, hooked a bull trout on the tail fly and then hooked a bat on the dropper!

With the help of 'two of the most successful anglers of the North Tyne' Chapman produced a recipe for successful bull/sea-trout fishing. They considered it essential not to disturb the water until 'the sun is well off it, and never before

6 P.M.' It was suggested that the angler should make up three casts of different sizes before he came to the river 'so as to be able quickly to change the smallest flies for larger as darkness deepens'. The third cast was for night use and should have 'fairly large flies, and these of lighter colour'. The droppers of all the flies should be fixed on short lengths of cast of some two inches. In strong water the angler was recommended to cast more directly downstream 'than is usual in salmon-fishing' and to work the flies very gently, bringing them slowly across the current and letting them 'hang' in the water. The angler should 'reel up at intervals after dusk, to see that all is clear and in order. When a fish comes strike quite deliberately, and never till you have felt him.'

Abel Chapman observed that the bull trout spawned earlier than the salmon, often during October, and returned to the main river in as little time as three weeks. If there was too little water in the burns the bull trout would spawn in the main river, near the salmon redds, but were always careful to avoid spots 'which are likely to be used later on by their cousins'. It is now known that the sea trout will spawn on finer gravel than salmon. In the first edition of *The Borders and Beyond* Chapman argued that sea trout never fed in fresh water, a view he changed in the second edition. It is also now known that sea trout do feed intermittently in fresh water, often at night, depending on food supply. Recent research has found that the sea trout does not stay long in the river after spawning, and that it may return to a river a number of times to spawn – there are records of fish that have spawned twelve times (Mills).

The main salmon runs in the North Tyne were August, September and October, but they could occur at any time of the year. Chapman had a theory that fish ran up the rivers for two reasons: in the autumn to spawn, and at any time of the year because of 'sea-satiety'. The salmon was so full of sea food, he argued, that it could 'gorge no more' and so, satiated, it returned to fresh water.

Chapman spent years studying the spawning salmon in the Houxty Burn and in the main river near his house. He became attached to them, even giving them names. On 4 January 1917 he noticed a 'great cock fish . . . in extremis', rolling over and over as the current carried it slowly down a large pool towards the watching Chapman. At that moment 'a faithful consort

BULL-TROUT AND SEA-TROUT.

Chapman's bull and sea trouts. FROM TOP TO BOTTOM: *bull trout, 5¾lb, Norway; bull trout, 4½lb, North Tyne; sea trout, 2lb 9oz, North Tyne; sea trout, 2½lb, North Tyne; sea trout, 2lb 1oz, North Uist.*

(hitherto unseen) sidled across from the darker depths of beyond and, I thought, whispered in his ear – had he possessed such an organ – "Come away 'Jim' I suspect danger lurking among these alders." Wearily the great tail got in action and the pair moved away from sight.'

The next day he was horrified to see another cock fish, that he had been observing at some length and had named Jack, 'stranded on the shoaling gravel of his bridal pool and a great encrimsoned gap yawned across his shoulder. During the night an otter had got him . . .' Jack had paired up with 'Jill', and Chapman had noticed that, unaided, Jill had dug the trenches in the river bed for her eggs. Jack waited patiently

some distance away and when the trench was ready he swam over, gently pushed Jill clear, and released a cloud of sperm over the eggs. The fertilised eggs were covered by Jill when she dug out the next trench upstream. The hen salmon in Houxty Burn each made as many as six 'nests' a day. Chapman noted that on the redds North Tyne salmon were usually monogamous, provided there were equal numbers of males and females on the redds, but should a 'serious sex-disparity occur (especially a redundant femininity) then rules are relaxed and promiscuity may prevail'.

On the evening of Abel Chapman's seventy-seventh birthday, just two years before he died, he went fishing in the North Tyne near Houxty,

TOP LEFT: *In extremis, Houxty Burn, 4 January, 1917.*
TOP RIGHT: *The midnight massacre, Houxty Burn, 4 January, 1917.*

BOTTOM LEFT: *The next morning, Houxty Burn, 5 January, 1917.*
BOTTOM RIGHT: *The midnight marauder, Houxty Burn, 1917.*

having already accounted for nine grouse and two blackcocks in 14 shots earlier that day. About half-way down Gold Islands streams a large salmon dashed across the river to take his Jock Scott, and after 20 minutes of 'pully-hauly' he landed a 'noble fish of exactly 25 lb'. After a few more casts there was another strong pull, a firm hold, and some 18 minutes later an 18½-lb. fish was on the bank. Wondering if he had the strength to continue, he suddenly saw a huge fish rise and heard the keeper muttering aghast, 'Man! Yon's a fifty-pounder!' Chapman reeled in, waded ashore and went home. In his own words, 'Now perhaps that last is an achievement unparalleled in the record of the World?'

He died in the house he had built in January 1929 and was buried in Wark churchyard less than half a mile away. On a cold January day in 1989 I stood by his grave. The site is now neglected and overgrown. The Kirk Burn and the North Tyne were in flood and so close that I could hear the sound of rushing water, carried by a raw, north-east wind. I found it easy to imagine the burial scene that took place exactly 60 years before and heard, in the wind blowing around the gravestones, the lament 'The Flowers of the Forest' that was played at his graveside on the Northumbrian small pipes by one of his oldest friends.

Below Houxty is Chipchase Castle, once a tower-castle or 'pele'. Chipchase was a typical mid-fourteenth-century pele, and they were common features of this landscape during the three centuries of border strife. It was the home of the Keeper of Tynedale whose role was to protect the dale against the Scots and to maintain law and order – an almost impossible task. A mansion was added to the pele in the seventeenth century and in the eighteenth century the tower and the mansion were further expanded and windowed.

Chipchase Castle has one of the best beats on the Tyne and it was fished by the river's most successful fishermen, T. Taylor and his son T. G. Taylor. In the castle library are a number of beautifully bound and immaculately kept salmon fishing records, beginning with the year 1882. Both Taylors kept their own books and there are four Chipchase Castle 'Salmon Books' summarising all the fish caught by father and son and their friends. They fished a two-and-a-half-mile stretch of the North Tyne which had 18 excellent pools – the Straits, Rocks, Parker's pool, Strother, Katherine's pool, Boat pool, Mill Stream, Burnfoot and Gullet, to name a few – and from 1884 to 1904 the stretch produced on average some 100 salmon and grilse each year. One of the best years was 1885 when 391 fish weighing 3042 lb. were caught. That year the best beat was the Straits where 68 salmon (average weight 11 lb.) and 97 grilse (average weight 6 lb.) were taken. The favourite salmon flies on the Chipchase water when the Taylors were fishing were Wilkinson, Greenwell, Silver Grey, Jock Scott, Sir Richard and a Stevenson. The most successful fly was the Wilkinson.

The best months for sea trout on the Chipchase water were July and August. And then the most successful sea-trout flies were dressed with either a claret body and mallard wing or a yellow body and a light drake wing.

Some of T. Taylor's salmon catches were remarkable:

1885	13.October (Straits)	18 fish = 117 lb.
1886	15 September (Straits)	10 fish = 103 lb.
1890	6 October (Rocks and Straits)	7 fish = 79 lb.

1891   9 October   11 fish = 149 lb.
      (Rocks)
1894   17 October   9 fish = 61 lb.
      (Straits and Rocks)
1900   15 October   7 fish = 112 lb.
1903   19 October   5 fish = 72 lb.
1912   26 August   6 fish = 86½ lb.
      (Straits)
1925   25 September   9 fish = 44½ lb.
      (Straits)
1926   29 October   6 fish = 97½ lb.

There was probably a keen rivalry between father and son, both being superb fishermen with time on their hands, and the Salmon Books continuously note their relative catches. In 1926, for example, it records that T. Taylor caught 141 salmon, average weight 13 lb., in 118 days, including evenings; while T. G. Taylor had 132 salmon, average weight 13⅔ lb., in 43 days including evenings. Generally T. caught more fish than T. G., but then he usually fished for longer.

In 1930 the largest recorded rod-caught salmon for the Tyne was taken. The Chipchase Salmon Book No. 4 notes that on 5 October there was a 4-foot flood and that two days later the water was still 11½ inches high. The seventh of October 1930 was a dull day with a westerly wind. 'T. T.' fished only in the afternoon. It was T. G. Taylor who cast into the Mill Stream with a number 12 double-hooked Durham Ranger tied to a 5/5 Hardy Brothers' light salmon cast and caught the record fish: a 42-lb. male salmon, girth 23¾

T. G. Taylor landing his son's first salmon. Chipchase water, Straits pool, c. 1920.

inches, length 49 inches spread of tail (unstretched) 11¼ inches. The book records it as a 'Kipper' but it was in good condition, giving 'a splendid fight and took just under 13 minutes to land' (letter to the *Newcastle Journal* from Lieut.- Colonel T. G. Taylor, 9 October 1930). Today a wooden replica of this magnificent fish is hung on the wall of the entrance room to the castle. In the year the record fish was taken, R. Taylor, T. G.'s son, appears in the Salmon Book. On 25 September 1930 R. Taylor caught a 6-lb. grilse and the next day an 18-lb. salmon. (At the age of ten, in 1922, R. Taylor had already caught a 25½-lb. spring salmon from Hendersyde Park on the Tweed; it was the heaviest fish of the season.)

Chipchase Castle Salmon Book No. 4 announces that 1937 was T. Taylor's seventy-fourth season, and that year he caught only one salmon (T. G. caught two). Sadly, after 1937 there are no more entries for T. Taylor. The water was let in 1938 and in 1939 T. G. Taylor was fishing without his father. He summarised the 1939 fishing as 'another disastrous season. No fish seen.' The river was dead.

Today the river has recovered and the Chipchase beat is now over four miles long. The Morrison-Bells lease some of their fishing, and in 1988 121 salmon and 185 sea trout were taken from the Chipchase water. Salmon Book No. 4 is being taken off its shelf again.

About two miles below Chipchase Castle and on the other side of the river is Haughton Castle, opposite the old North British Railway station at Barrasford. The fishing here and elsewhere on the North Tyne is owned and fished by local landowners and farmers or leased from them by syndicates or local angling clubs. But as the river approaches Chollerford, another station on the old railway line and the site of an important Roman bridge, there is fishing for the visiting angler. Upstream of Chollerford Bridge, for three-quarters of a mile and on either side of the river, the fishing is owned by the George Hotel. The George has been there for over 250 years, and in 1882 W. J. Palmer wrote about a 'comfortable inn near the bridge [that] has no doubt often afforded refreshment to the itinerant bent on a survey of the Roman Wall'. The George continues to afford refreshment and also provides free salmon fishing for guests. In the last week of the 1989 season a 27½-lb., a 12½-lb. and two 8-lb. salmon were caught.

In the past, salmon fishing on this section of the river yielded large fish. In 1927 a local newspaper reported that 'fishing in the North Tyne between Chollerford and Barrasford, Mr Wallace Watson, of Black Hall, landed a salmon which turned the scale at 40 lb. It was a female fish, 50¾ in. long and the girth was 24½ in. It is the biggest fish recorded even in this memorable season, and is probably the biggest landed in the North Tyne for some years.' (22 October 1927; George Bolam.)

Below Chollerford is the village of Wall, close to the point where Hadrian's Wall crossed the North Tyne and once the first station on the North British Railway Company's line after Hexham Bridge. The railway ran close to the river bank and fishermen nowadays use the trackway as a path. Ken Muter is one of these anglers and often imagines the old steam trains working their way up to the headwaters of the North Tyne. He fishes the stretch of water that runs up from the confluence of the North and South Tynes and is controlled by the Tyne Watersmeet Fishery. Besides being a management committee member of the fishery, he is also a National Anglers' Council grade I game-angling and fly-dressing instructor. Each year he runs a night class in fly dressing; it is always well attended, and during it he usually explains how his fishing techniques have changed over the years. 'When I was young I'd arrive at the water's edge, desperate to go fishing. I'd tackle up my trout rod, tie on a Greenwell's Glory, rush down to the water's edge, and start thrashing the water. Nowadays I arrive, I take my time tackling up, I sit for half an hour by the water's edge, all the while examining the fly life, the lies, the nature of the rises, and think about which of my dozens of flies to use. Then I reach into the box, tie on a Greenwell's Glory and start thrashing the water!'

This is an exaggeration. Ken Muter does not 'thrash the water'; in fact he teaches casting to both trout and salmon anglers, and to see him deliver a salmon fly is to witness the art of fly casting. Despite all his skills, like most anglers, he does not always catch fish. 'I believe it is 80 per cent salmon, 20 per cent fisherman which brings the fish to the fly,' he says.

Ken Muter is a member of the Fly Dressers' Guild. He dresses both tube flies and Waddingtons for salmon fishing in cold, heavy, spring and autumn Tyne waters, and prefers tube flies to Waddingtons. 'If the Waddington's hook becomes damaged, it's the end of it, but with a tube fly you just change the hook.' He fishes with treble rather than double hooks, believing they are more reliable, and fishes with a size 8, 6 or 4 hook depending on the water conditions. He uses modern hairwing dressings on long-shanked hooks but can, of course, tie beautiful traditional flies. The fly he uses most in the Tyne is the Willie Gunn, dressed as follows:

Body: Black floss silk
Rib: Flat gold tinsel
Wing: Orange bucktail under yellow bucktail
    under black bucktail tied around the shank.

He varies the relative amounts of orange, black and yellow bucktail, increasing the amount of black bucktail for clear water conditions. All his flies are works of art, especially the Willie Gunns. They lie in the fly box in closely compacted rows, like ranks of painted toy soldiers, their colours gradually changing from bright yellow/orange (for coloured water) to almost black.

If the river is very low and clear he uses a Stoat's Tail:

Tag: Oval silver tinsel
Tail: Golden pheasant crest
Body: Black floss silk
Rib: Oval silver tinsel
Hackle: Black cock
Wing: Stoat tail or black squirrel.

And if the Tyne is fast and very coloured, or if he is fishing fast, turbulent water he uses a simplified version of a Silver Doctor:

Butt: Red wool
Body: Flat silver tinsel
Hackle: Pale blue cock hackle and widgeon
Wing: Red bucktail under yellow bucktail
Head: Red

He always carries a thermometer and at around
48°F fishes a floating line. He decreases the size of
the fly as the temperature of the water increases,
using the following table as a general guide:

35°–40°F 2½ to 3-inch Waddington (or tube
   fly)
40°–45°F 2 to 3-inch Waddington (or tube fly)
45°–50°F size 4 to 6 long-shanked trebles
50°–55°F size 6 to 8 long-shanked trebles
55°–60°F size 8 to 10 long-shanked trebles

'Hud'.

North Tyne fishing hut.

When choosing a fly, however, he mainly picks one that 'feels right'. He does this by dangling his first choice in the water close to his feet and observing its behaviour. 'Such a basis for choosing a fly is very difficult to describe. Confidence in a fly, believing you have chosen correctly, has a marked effect on casting and presentation, resulting in the all-important factor of putting the fly at the right depth, speed and position relative to a taking fish. Having achieved this, the pattern and size are of lesser importance,' says Ken Muter. Recently he has been tying salmon flies on weighted number 12 long-shanked sea-trout hooks and has caught large autumn-run salmon on the North Tyne.

Another member of the Tyne Watersmeet Fishery is Paul Huddleston. He is one of the oldest salmon fishers on Tyne Waters. At 74 he finally abandoned heavy fibreglass rods for carbon fibre, and now uses a 15-foot carbon rod with a 9-foot, 15-lb. nylon cast attached in spring and autumn to a number 10 Wet Cel sinking line. In the summer when the river is low he changes to an Air Cel floating line. He dresses his own flies and usually uses only one pattern and size – a Stinchar's Stoat's Tail on a number 8 hook – and catches lots of fish. Recently Guy Hall gave him a fly that he had rejected. With it Hud caught six salmon on five different rivers in three countries – England, Scotland and Ireland.

Hud's 80 years have seen many changes on the Tyne. Mighty industrial Tyneside has faded, but its river, once a black open sewer, is clean again. Just below the beat he fishes the North and South Tynes meet and become one. In 1882 Palmer described this marriage of the Tynes:

South Tyne, a son of toil, from fountain-head and earliest springs associated with mines; and beautiful North Tyne, a daughter of the moors, is she not known as the brightness of the smiling haughs, and the joy of flocks which come down to her at noon? Well! under Warden Hill, these two streams become one; they came swiftly and joyously to their union, but now take a more dignified pace, flowing at leisure past Hexham's ancient towers, by Beaufront, Dilston, Corbridge, and the green lawns of Bywell, soon, however, to resume work – increasing work – of pastoral service less and less, and finally there remains for Coaly Tyne but one long working day, midst smoking chimneys, blazing furnaces, and forests of masts, until it reaches THE SEA.

The smoking chimneys, the blazing furnaces, the forests of masts have all gone and Coaly Tyne is no more. But from the sea the salmon are returning and – if we do not prevent it – in ever-increasing numbers.

Select Bibliography

Bolam, G., 'The Fishes of Northumberland and the Eastern Borders', *The History of the Berwickshire Naturalists' Club*, 23 (1916–1918) pp. 153–97 and 250–304.

Bradley, A. G. *The Romance of Northumberland*, Methuen, London, 1908.

Brand, J., *The History and Antiquities of the Town and County of Newcastle upon Tyne*, 2 vols., London, 1789.

British Association for the Advancement of Science, *Scientific Survey of North-Eastern England*, Newcastle, 1949.

Carmichael, J. W., *Pictures of Tyneside or Life and Scenery on the River Tyne*, c. 1830, Newcastle.

Chapman, A. *Wild Norway*, London, 1897. *Bird-Life of the Borders*, 2nd edn. London, 1907. *The Borders and Beyond*, London, 1924. *Memories of Fourscore Years less Two. 1851–1929*, London, 1930.

Charlton, B., *Upper North Tynedale*, Northumbrian Water, Newcastle, 1987. *The Story of Redesdale*, Northumberland County Council, Gateshead, 1986.

Chaytor, A. H., *Letters to a Salmon Fisher's Sons*, André Deutsch, London, 1910. *Essays Sporting and Serious*, London, 1930.

Davis, R., *The Rise of the English Shipping Industry*, David and Charles, Newton Abbot, 1962.

Durham Household Book, The Surtees Society, London, 1844.

Finch, R., *Coals from Newcastle*, T. Dalton, Lavenham, 1973.

Francis, Francis, *A Book on Angling* (1867), 7th edn (ed. Herbert Maxwell), London, 1920.

Gardiner, R., *England's Grievances Discovered in relation to the Coal Trade*, London, 1655.

Grimble, A., *The Salmon Rivers of England and Wales*, Kegan Paul, Trench, Trubner and Co., London, 1904 and 1913.

Gutherie, J., *The River Tyne*, A. Reid and Co., Newcastle, 1880.

Harbottle, J., *A Fisher's Garland*, Chorley and Pickersgill, Leeds, 1904.

Hartley, B., and Fitts, L., *The Brigantes*, A. Sutton, Gloucester, 1988.

Hepple, L. W., *A History of Northumberland and Newcastle upon Tyne*, Phillimore and Co., Chichester, 1976.

Hodgson, G. B., *The History of South Shields*, A. Reid and Co., Newcastle, 1924.

Hofland, T. C., *The British Anglers Manual*, H. G. Bohn, London, 1839 and 1848.

Hopper, R., Letter dated 1 November 1834, Northumberland County Record Office.

Johnson, R. W., *The Making of the Tyne. A Record of Fifty Years' Progress*, Walter Scott Ltd, London and Newcastle, 1895.

Johnson, R. W. and Aughton, R. (eds.), *The River Tyne, Its Trade and Facilities*, Andrew Reid and Co., Newcastle, 1934.

McAllum, W. F., *Salmon and Trout Rivers and Their Improvement*, Gateshead, 1892.

Mackenzie, E., *A Descriptive and Historical Account of the Town and County of Newcastle upon Tyne, including the Borough of Gateshead*, Newcastle, 1827.

Macklin, M. G., and Dowsett, R. B., 'The chemical and physical speciation of trace metals in fine-grained, over-bank flood sediments in the Tyne basin, North-East England', *Catena 16*, no. 2 (1989), pp. 135–51.

Marshall, M. W., *Fishing: the Coastal Tradition*, Batsford, London, 1987.

Marson, C. M. D., *Fishing for Salmon*, A. & C. Black, London, 1929.

Maxwell, H., *Post Meridiana: Afternoon Essays*, London, 1895.
Salmon and Sea Trout, London, 1898.

Menzies, W. J. M., *The Salmon: Its Life Story*, William Blackwood and Sons, Edinburgh and London, 1925.

Middlebrook, S., *Newcastle upon Tyne, Its Growth and Achievement*, Newcastle Journal, Newcastle, 1950.

Mills, D., *Salmon and Sea Trout*, Oliver and Boyd, Edinburgh, 1971.

Oglesby, A., *Salmon*, Macdonald and Co., London, 1986.

Oliver, S., *Scenes and Recollections of Fly Fishing*, Chapman and Hall, London, 1834.
Rambles in Northumberland and on the Scottish Border, London, 1835.

Palmer, W. J., *The Tyne and its Tributaries*, George Bell and Sons, London, 1882.

Raistrick, A., and Jennings, B., *A History of Lead Mining in the Pennines*, Longmans, London, 1965.

Rennison, R. W., *Water to Tyneside. A History of Newcastle and Gateshead Water Company*, Northumberland Press, 1979.

Rivet, A., and Smith, C., *The Place Names of Roman Britain*, Batsford, London, 1979.

Robinson, R., *Thomas Bewick. His Life and Times*, F. Graham, Newcastle, 1887 and 1972.

Runciman, J., *The Romance of the Coast*, George Bull & Sons, 1883.

Smith, L. A., *Music of the Waters*, Kegan Paul, Trench and Co., Newcastle, 1888.

Sykes, J., *Local Records or Historical Register of Remarkable Events*, vols. I and II, 1833. Reprinted T. Fordyce, Newcastle, 1866.

Taverner, E., *Salmon Fishing*, London, 1931.

Tomlinson, W. W., *Life in Northumberland during the sixteenth century*, London, 1897.

TJSB (Tyneside Joint Sewerage Board) 1966–1974, *The Polluted Tyne*.

Walton, I., *The Compleat Angler*, London, 1653.

Watson, G., *The Border Reivers*, Sandhill Press, Alnwick, 1988.

Welford, R., *History of Newcastle and Gateshead*, Walter Scott Ltd, London and Newcastle upon Tyne, 1881.

Wheeler, A., *The Tidal Thames*, London, 1979.

Appendix
WHERE TO FISH

Close Season

Salmon: 1 November–31 January incl.
Sea trout: 1 November–2 April incl.
Brown trout: 1 October–21 March incl.
Reservoirs: 1 November–30 April incl.

Where to fish, permits and information for:

I *The main Tyne*

Hexham, Tyne Green: Hexham Tourist Centre,
  Hexham House, Gilesgate, Hexham
Ovingham and Wylam: Northumbrian Anglers'
  Federation, The Head Bailiff, Thirston Mill,
  West Thirston, Felton, Morpeth

Fishermen's Information Service, National Rivers
  Authority, Northumbria Region:
Northern Area 091 213 0828
Southern Area 091 213 0829

To report chemical or oil spillages, pollution
  incidents, fish kills or poaching, ring the
  24-hour emergency service: 091 213 0266.

II *South Tyne*

Haltwhistle and District Angling Association: c/o
  Greggs Sports Shop, Main Street, Haltwhistle
South Tyne Angling Club: c/o 24 Strother Close,
  Haydon Bridge
Allendale Angling Association (East Allen):
  Allendale Post Office, Allendale
Alston and District Angling Association: A. and
  P. Struthers, Front Street, Alston

III *North Tyne*

Kielder and Bakethin Reservoirs: Matthews Linn
  Fishing Base, Kielder Water
Falstone Fishing Club: c/o Black Cock Inn,
  Falstone
Riverdale Hall Hotel, Bellingham
George Hotel, Chollerford

IV *River Rede*

Otterburn Towers Hotel, Otterburn
Percy Arms Hotel, Otterburn

Index

Figures in italics refer to pages with illustrations.

Aethelfrith, 16
Agricola, Julius, 13, 15
Allen, R., 126
Allendale Angling Association, 123
Allgood, Capt. A. G., 145
Alston and District Angling Association, 123, 127
Alston Angling Club, 127
Anglers' Co-operative Association, 115
angling *see* fishing methods
Anglo-Saxons, 16–17
Appleby, Sid, 86
Ashley-Cooper, John, 106
Associations for the Prevention of Poaching, 43
Atkinson, Maynard, 96–7

bailiffs, 52, 68–9, 72, 77–9, 96, 107–9
Bakethin Reservoir, 74–5, 133
Balfour-Kinnear, G. P. R., 121
Baliol, Sir John de, 95
Beaumont family, 114, 133
Bede, 17
Begg, Dr, 120, 140
Bewick, Thomas, 23, *24*, *25*, 91, 95
Blackett, Christopher, 87, 88
Blackett family, 114
Blaydon Salmon Fishery, 49
Boarg, Capt., 87

boats: cobles, 44, *45*, 68; colliers, *23*, 36, *37*, 38, 60; coracles, 16; dredgers, *27*, 38–9; foyboats, 60; keels, *23*, 36; trows, *129*, 135–6
Bolam, George, 46, 106, 113, 114, 124–6, 142, 143, 150
Boyle, W., 93
Bradley, A. G., 56, 106, 111, 142
Brand, Revd John, 13, 15, 22
bridges, 13–15, 17, 29–30, *29*, *31*, 39, 65
British Field Sport Society, 61
British Rail, 88
Broust-Cocker, Iben, 136
Brown, John Stoker, 56
bull trout, 145–6, *146*

Carmichael, John W., *23*, *34–5*
Catcleugh Reservoir, 138–9, *138*
Chadwick Report, 59
Chapman, Abel, 106, 124, 142–8, *145*
Charlton, B., 131, 134, 138
Charlton, William Henry, 133
Chatto, William Andrew *see* Oliver, Stephen
Chaytor, A. H., 83, 85–6, 97, 99–100, 102, 104–6, 109
Chaytor family, 98, 99
Cheeseman, James, 59
coal, 17, 19–20, 21, 29, 36–7
Cocker, John, 136
Cookson, Colonel Fife, 142
Coquet anglers, 92
Corbridge Riverside Sport Club, 102, 120
Coxon, J. L., 61
Crawford (bailiff), 52

Dagg, Thomas, 56
Davis, R., 36
Dawson, Councillor G., 115
Defoe, Daniel, 21, 22

Dowsett, R. B., 115
Drewett, Drewett Ormond, 99, 102
Dunn, Commander, 95
Durham, bishops of, 17–21, 113
Durham, priors of, 17, 19

Earsman, Gordon, 73–7, *74*, 79, 133
Edward III, King, 20
Edward VIII, King, 30
Egbert, king of Wessex, 17
Elizabeth I, Queen, 21, 95

Falstone Fishing Club, 134
Fife, Sir Aubone, 142
Fishery Board, 61
fishing methods: dibbling, 120–1, *121*; draft nets, 46–52, 67, 86; drift nets, 44–6, *45*, 67, 68; flies, 23, 87, 90, 97, 99–105, 107, 109, 117–20, 146, 148, 151–4; history, 16, 20–3, 32, 41–2; lines, 117–19; rods, 23, 84, 86, 97, 109, 117–19, 127; spearing, *129*, 135–6; *see also* poaching
fishmongers, 46, 51, 52, 86, 106, 108
Fitts, L., 16
Fly Dressers' Guild, 151
Forestry Commission, 132
Forster, Robert, 41
Foster, Bob, 48
Foster, 'Dutcher', 49
Foster family, 49
Francis, Francis, 104, 105, 106

Gardiner, Ralph, 21, *22*, 38
Gibson, Charles, 95
Gill, Tom, 125
Gillender, Neil, 126–7
Gracie, Major J. T., 108
gravel removal, 108

Gray (local historian), 21
Gray, Peter, *70*, 72–9
Grey, Sir Edward, 94
Grimble, Augustus, 42–6, 113, 135, 142
Gutherie, J., 18

Hadrian, 13–14, 15
Hagan, J., 89
Halfdan, 17
Hall, Guy, 120–1, *121*, 123, 154
Hall, James, 132–3, *132*
Hall, Jonathan, 134
Hall, 'Mad Jack', 137
Hall, Robert, 132–3
Haltwhistle and District Angling Club, 123
Haltwhistle Rural Council, 115
Harbottle, John, 93, 94
Harbottle, Sergeant, 44
Hardy's of Alnwick, 118
Hartley, B., 16
hatcheries, 92, 108, *see also* Kielder Hatchery
Hatcheries Committee, 92
Henry II, King, 18
Henry IV, King, 20
Henry VIII, King, 20, 131
Hexham Angling Club, 91, 107
Hexham Local Board of Health, 43
Hexham Rural Council, 115
Hindmarch (Houxty estate keeper), 106
Hodgson, G. B., 38
Hofland, T. C., 32
Honorius, 16
Hopper, R., 43
Hostmen, Newcastle Company of, 21, 36
Huddlestone, Paul, *152*, 154
Hunter, Mr, 113

Izaak Walton angling club, 91

Jackson, Billy, 96
James, R., 86
Jennings, B., 114
Johnson, R. W., 33, 39
Jordon, R., 113

Keelmen, Society of, 36
Kielder Hatchery, 69–79, *70–1*
Kielder Reservoir, 11, 47, 69–72, *69*, 118, 132–4

Larcomba, Frank, 56
lead mines, 17, 20, 42, 43, 113–15

McAllum, W. F., 56
McCredie, Ian, 116–20
Mackenzie, E., 32
Macklin, M. G., 115
McLoughlan family, 49
March, David, 115
Marson, Cyril, 106
Maxwell, Sir Herbert, 104–6, 120, 139–40, 143
Milburn (fishmonger), 106
Mills, D., 146
Ministry of Agriculture, Fisheries and Food, 61
Mitchell, William, 33
Morrison-Bell family, 150
Muter, Ken, 150–1, *151*, 154

National Anglers' Council, 150
National Rivers Authority, 64, 68, 69, 77, 108
nets *see* fishing methods
Nevill, Ralph de, 95
Newbrough and Fourstones Angling Club, 123
Newcastle and Gateshead Water Company, 43, 61, 138, 139
Newcastle angling club, 56
Newcastle Company of Hostmen, 21, 36
Newcastle Waltonian Club, 33

Nichol, Derek, 127
Nichol, Robert, 33
North British Railway Company, 92, 132, 133, 136, 150
North Tyne and Reedwater Association, 134
Northern angling club, 91
Northumberland and Tyneside River Board, 61, 108, 115
Northumberland Angling Club, 93–4, *93*, 94
Northumberland, Dukes of, 41, 49, 92, 94–5, 131–4, 139
Northumberland, Earl of, 95
Northumbrian Anglers' Federation, 64, 83, 87, 91, 92–6, *92*, 99, 107; *Handbook and Guide*, 61–4, 91, 117
Northumbrian River Authority, 86, 108
Northumbrian Water Authority, 64–5, 73, 77, 108

Oglesby, Arthur, 106, 117
Oliver, Stephen (William Andrew Chatto), 32, 104, 134–6

Palmer, W. J., 16, 33, 43, 124, 132–4, 136, 150, 154
Percy, Henry, 95
Percy, Lord, 105
Percy, Sir William, 131
Pliny the Elder, 16
poaching, 42–4, 56, 68–9, 77–9, 91–2, 94, 108–9, 134
Pollard, Kit, 88
pollution, 42–3, 56, 94, 108, 113–15, *see also* sewage
Ptolemy, 13
Public Health Act (1875), 60

railways, 29, 92, 113, 114, 127, 133

Raistrick, A., 114
Rea, J. S., 93–4, *93*
reivers, 131, 137
Rennison, R. W., 56, 59–60, 139
Reynolds, W., *94*
Richard II, King, 95
Ripley, James, 56
Rivers Pollution Prevention Act (1876), 60, 61
Robert, duke of Normandy, 17
Robertson, John, 117
Robinson, M., 113
Robinson, Robert, 23
Robson, A., 106
Roman occupation, 13–16
Runciman, J., 44

Sally the Mugger, 138
salmon: grilse, 57, 136; kelts, 51–2, 75, 144–5; parr, 57, 86, 134–5; smolts, 57, 86; spawning, 146–7; *see also* fishing methods, hatcheries, poaching
Salmon Conservancy Board, 93
salmon fisheries, 18–19, 22, 30, 41, 46, 46–7, 48–52, *48, 50*
Salmon Fishery Acts (1861–5), 41, 42, 61, 91
salt, 20
Scott, Archie, 49
Scott, George, 49
Scott, Henry, 41
Scott, Joss, 49
Scott, Ken, 109
sea trout, 74–5, 79, 121, 123, 127, 133, 145–6, *146*, 148
Sealey's (rods), 118
sewage, 40, 43, 56, 59–65, 107
Sewerage Board, 64
Smith, Laura Alexandrine, 9

South Tyne Angling Club, 123
Sowerby, Andrew, *100–1*
Stephenson, George, 29, 33, 86
Stephenson, Robert, 30
Stoddart, George, 56
Stokoe, Jimmy, 46, 48, 51
Stokoe, Robert, 46–7, 49–52, 56
Stokoe, Walter, 46–51
Sutterby, Rod, 123–4
Sykes, J., 22, 32

Taverner, Eric, 99
Taylor, R., *149*, 150
Taylor, Thomas, 145, 148–50
Taylor, T. G., 148–50
Thompson, William, 33, 82
Todd, R., 124
Tomlinson, W. W., 21
Turner, Dr William, 21
Tyne Committee, 92–3
Tyne Conservancy Board, 56
Tyne Fisheries Association, 43
Tyne Improvement Act (1857), 56
Tyne Improvement Commission, 38, 56
Tyne Navigation Act, 38
Tyne Port Health Authority, 61
Tyne River Police, 56
Tyne Salmon Conservancy, 94
Tyne Salmon Fishery Board, 43
Tyne Salmon Fishery District Board of Conservators, 41
Tyne Sewerage Committee, 61
Tyne Watersmeet Fishery, 150, 154
Tynedale District Council, 107
Tynemouth, prior of, 19, 20, 95
Tyneside Anglers' Federation, 91, 92
Tyneside Joint Sewerage Board (TJSB), 59, 60, 64

Tyneside Sewage Treatment Scheme, 64

Umphraville, Robert, Lord of Redesdale, 137
Ure, J. F., 38

Vaughan, W. S., 93–4, *93*
Victoria, Queen, 33, 46
Vies (Newcastle fishmonger), 51, 52
Vikings, 17

Waddington, Richard, 120
Walker, Keith, 96
Walker-Bampton, 118
Wallace, Alan, 86–7, *87*, 88–90, 107
Wallace family, 49
Walton, Hugh, 124
Walton, Izaak, 23
Walton, Joe, 126
Warden Paper Mill Dam, 113–14
Water Resources Act (1963), 64
Watson, G., 131
Watson, James, 107–9
Watson, R., 113
Watson, Wallace, 150
Wealans, 'Big Jack', 48
Welford, R., 19, 21
West End Anglers, 91
Westmorland, Earls of, 95
Wheeler, A., 25
Wilkinson, Jackie, 86
Wilkinson, 'Ossie', 86
William the Conqueror, 15, 137
Wordsworth, William, 16
Wylam Angling Club, 83, 86–90

Young, J. W., 118